Leading Together

Leading Together

Unlocking Relational Leadership Mastery

Rocky Bandzeladze

BEP

BUSINESS EXPERT PRESS

Leader in applied, concise business books

Leading Together: Unlocking Relational Leadership Mastery

First published in 2025 by
Business Expert Press, LLC
222 East 46th Street, New York, NY 10017
www.businessexpertpress.com

ISBN-13: 978-1-63742-796-5 (paperback)
ISBN-13: 978-1-63742-797-2 (e-book)

Business Expert Press Human Resource Management and Organizational
Behavior Collection

First edition: 2025

10 9 8 7 6 5 4 3 2 1

EU SAFETY REPRESENTATIVE
Mare Nostrum Group B.V.
Mauritskade 21D
1091 GC Amsterdam
The Netherlands
gpsr@mare-nostrum.co.uk

Growing up in the middle of the Civil War in the Republic of Georgia, I remember my father giving me $1,500 from the sale of our only family asset, our car, to buy a plane ticket to come to the United States. The plan was to get a good education and find a better life to support my family eventually. So, here I was at the age of 19, entering JFK Airport with $180 in my pocket, money left over from the sale of my father's car after I bought the plane ticket. The suffocating heat of that hot New York summer day still lingers in my memory, a stark contrast to the cold uncertainty I felt inside. I was alone in a foreign land, with no option to turn back, knowing my family's hopes rested on my shoulders. Yet, instead of fear, I was filled with a sense of excitement and purpose, fueled by my father's parting words: "I expect great things from you." My parents had given me everything they had; now, it was my turn to make good on their faith.

For the next three years, I worked tirelessly—moving furniture, stocking shelves at K-Mart, pulling graveyard shifts at fast-food joints—logging 80- to 100-hour weeks to save enough for community college. The cultural adjustment was challenging but it paled in comparison to the determination driving me forward. Over time, I graduated with a bachelor's degree in economics, followed by an MBA, and finally, a doctorate in Organizational Leadership. My professional journey has been nothing short of extraordinary over the past thirty years, leading large financial organizations and launching start-ups, most recently Agora Space Technologies, a pioneering aerospace engineering, component design, and FAA certification company. Today, I'm blessed to live in sunny Orange County with a wonderful family: my beautiful wife, our 11-year-old twins, and a loving Goldendoodle puppy. Every day, I remind myself how fortunate I am to have this life and to live in this amazing country.

It may seem unusual to speak of myself in a dedication meant for others, but I wanted to provide the proper context for what I'm about to say. Every achievement and success I've enjoyed is not just a reflection of my efforts but of the incredible people who have supported and guided me along the way.

To my parents, who sacrificed so much for the life I've been able to build; to my sister, who has been the strength of our family since my departure from Georgia; to Alina Henderson, who inspired me to come to the United States in pursuit of education; to Barbara Zirino, who welcomed me into her family and supported me in my early years here; to Marco Zirino, who was a kind and wise brother and taught me to stay true to my Christian values amidst the world's distractions; to the Gillett family, who became my second family during my community college days; to Dr. Betty Uribe, who recognized my potential, entrusted me with my first Senior V.P. role, and has been a mentor ever since; to Ash Abdelaaty, a loyal and sage friend; to Dr. Lola Gershfeld, whose insights and encouragement motivated me to write about this topic; to Dr. Laura Hyatt, whose guidance as my dissertation chair helped shape my understanding of this subject and laid the foundation for this book; to my wife, Veronica, who has been the calm, supportive force behind my relentless pursuits; and to my twins, Michael and Emma, who have given my life its truest purpose. My deepest gratitude to each and every one of you. You are the catalysts for the relational leadership concept that inspired this book.

Description

Leading Together: Unlocking Relational Leadership Mastery explores the profound shifts in workplace dynamics and leadership paradigms in the context of a volatile, uncertain, complex, and ambiguous world. The book delves into the evolution of leadership, highlighting how traditional hierarchical models are increasingly inadequate in addressing the complex challenges of modern organizations. Through a comprehensive examination of relational leadership theory, the book argues for a leadership approach that emphasizes collective efforts and deep, authentic relationships between leaders and followers.

The narrative is grounded in both rigorous academic research and real-world examples, offering a practical guide for leaders who seek to foster engaging, enduring, and high-performing organizational cultures. The relational leadership model proposed in this book moves beyond the archaic leader–follower manager–subordinate dynamics, advocating for leadership as a shared social process where the contributions of all members are equally valued.

In a world reshaped by the COVID-19 pandemic, rapid technological advancements, and changing generational labor preferences, *Leading Together: Unlocking Relational Leadership* Mastery provides essential insights for leaders who aim to navigate uncertainty, create positive, engaging workplace cultures, and achieve sustainable organizational success. This book is an invaluable resource for leaders and practitioners who are committed to enhancing personal and organizational effectiveness in today's ever-changing marketplace.

Contents

CHAPTER 1

What Is Going On?

Since the dawn of the Industrial Revolution, the workplace dynamics between employers and employees have undergone rapid transformation. What once began as a hierarchical and authoritarian relationship, with employers wielding significant power over their workforce, has gradually evolved into a more dynamic and complex interplay of roles and responsibilities. The rise of labor unions, legislations protecting workers' rights, technological advancements, changing generational labor preferences, and the competition for top talent in the marketplace have all contributed to this shift. These changes promoted both organizations and employees to reassess the entrenched norms and practices surrounding employee empowerment, engagement, talent retention, and cultivating a positive and high-performing workplace culture. However, recent negative labor trends have cast a shadow over this progress. The Great Resignation, Quiet Hiring, worsening employee engagement, the rise in toxic organizational cultures, and the loud outcry from employees about the lack of psychological safety at work are daily hot topics on media channels.

I recently came across a LinkedIn post mocking corporate executives who compare their workplaces to families. While the post itself was humorous, what struck me was the sheer volume of comments it generated. Thousands of people chimed in, sharing brief but intensely personal experiences about the lack of corporate loyalty while ridiculing the idea of organizations being compared to a family. The outcry was overwhelming. This example, alongside the prevalent negative trends reported daily in various media, underscores the growing disconnect between traditional leadership approaches and the evolving needs and expectations of today's workforce, which cannot be ignored.

The COVID-19 pandemic, which began in the United States on January 20, 2020 (Centers for Disease Control and Prevention 2022), further intensified already worsening labor relations, exposing vulnerabilities in traditional organizational leadership models and emphasizing the critical need to explore alternative approaches. With millions sick, hundreds of thousands of lives lost, a record number of businesses closed, and soaring unemployment, organizations across the country experienced an unprecedented disruption in how employees interacted with their leaders and each other and how organizational cultures were created and maintained.

The regulatory restrictions and concern for the spread of the virus in the workplace forced executives of many businesses to transition most of their employees to remote work arrangements. Company executives found themselves leading a predominantly remote workforce, which was a significant departure from the historical norm for many of them. Leaders could no longer capitalize on the personal connections forged through daily face-to-face interactions with employees. Instead, they had to resort to communicating via various teleconference platforms. This shift required executives to be more thoughtful in their daily engagement and communication approach, realizing that conducting meetings via teleconferencing provided a unique opportunity for participants to see each other in a home setting, often catching glimpses of each other's families, which necessitated a softer and more empathetic approach (Dewar et al. 2020). One Wall Street executive remarked:

> People are looking to me for a different kind of leadership. In a normal environment, it is about business leadership and setting up strategy, as well as culture and people decisions. In this environment, it is about helping people maintain morale. It is about people being prepared for whatever may come in the face of uncertainty (as cited in Dewar et al. 2020, 3).

If shareholder interest was always the first thought for CEOs, focusing on the employees' well-being became the top priority during the pandemic (Dewar et al. 2020). Executives were called upon to make decisions they were never trained for—tough leadership decisions with profound human consequences—such as how to manage the pandemic spread in the employee ranks when someone contracted the virus;

which groups of employees to deploy to interface with clients and thus exposing them to a higher chance of catching the virus; and when was it safe to return to offices. These changes have elevated people issues to the forefront of leaders' priorities.

The postpandemic environment introduced a new layer of challenges in the already changing leader–employee dynamics at the workplace. While most Americans expressed the preference for working remotely at least some of the days during the week (Barrero et al. 2021; Parker et al. 2020), many CEOs argued that employees' working from home is not practical for their organizations (The Wall Street Journal 2021). Numerous leaders contend that remote work prevents people in their organizations from collaborating effectively and building internal and external relationships necessary to develop and maintain organizational cultures (The Wall Street Journal 2021). As a result, many CEOs have mandated a total return to offices.

While both sides of the argument have merit, the complexity of determining which side is more compelling is beyond the scope of this book. However, what is undeniable is that the COVID-19 pandemic fundamentally accelerated shifting leader–employee dynamics at the workplace, specifically how leaders and employees interact, build relationships, and create engaging and performing organizational cultures. As a result, there is an ongoing dialogue in the business community and academia alike on the effectiveness of the remote workforce in building collaborative, engaging, and performing organizational cultures in the postpandemic era. However, what appears to need to be added in recent discourse is the focus on the leader's role and responsibility during these challenging times related to creating organizational environments where the company and its employees can thrive. If leaders of successful companies, where organizational cultures prosper and the company's financial performance exceeds expectations, are often credited for creating such positive environments conducive to success, why is the focus not on the lack or absence of leadership amidst the increasingly negative leader–follower trends?

It is particularly concerning that such a glaring absence of attention on leadership is occurring, given the overwhelming abundance of readily available literature detailing leaders' pivotal role in fostering trust-based, positive, engaging, and performing organizational cultures. Despite the vast repository of academic research and the multitude of leadership books flooding the market every year—Amazon alone boasts over 57,000 titles—the question remains: Why are we still grappling with pervasive issues such as employee disengagement and toxic cultures? Even the plethora of leadership training sessions conducted by Learning and Development (L&D) departments across the nation, promising to unveil the latest leadership techniques, fall short of addressing the core issues. While the efforts put forth by the L&D professionals are commendable, the stark reality is that these programs often fail to catalyze lasting change in leader–follower dynamics or foster enduring organizational cultures. Such persistent negative trends paint a disheartening picture of leadership's current state and underscore the urgent need for a paradigm shift.

Interestingly, and trying not to sound arrogant, my professional journey has unveiled a starkly contrasting narrative amidst the negativity surrounding organizational cultures. Don't get me wrong, indeed, like many people, I have experienced selfish, narcissistic, and even dishonorable bosses and worked through toxic organizational cultures. However, my professional experience has also uncovered overwhelmingly positive aspects of leadership that have consistently surprised me on both intellectual and emotional levels. The profound emotional bonds I observed between the leaders I had the privilege of knowing and collaborating with and their followers stood in stark contrast to the negative leader–follower dynamics mentioned earlier. These authentic connections drastically contrasted with the best practices of various leadership styles emphasized in corporate leadership training I have attended or the distinctive leadership theories I have studied. The capacity of these leaders to establish deep personal connections with those around them, resulting in unparalleled employee engagement, cohesion, high morale, and organizational performance, was truly extraordinary. It is paramount to note that while genuine, these leaders' actions were not without a degree of self-interest aimed at achieving top results for their organizations, nor were they devoid of external or internal competition for resources needed to accomplish their goals. The difference was that these leaders were able to create unique personal experiences with their followers and, together with them, create organizational cultures that enabled the organization and employees to thrive together.

I craved to study this phenomenon academically, attempting to connect various relational leadership theories with the practical, real-life leadership examples I had witnessed. Subsequently, during my doctoral studies, I encountered an emerging leadership theory known as Relational Leadership, which closely aligns with the positive real-life leadership practices I had experienced. However, I discovered that while numerous leadership books delve into specific relationship-based concepts, there is scant literature comprehensively addressing relational leadership theory and an almost nonexistent body of work that connects relational leadership theoretical models with real-life leadership practices. Subsequently, while acknowledging the irony of adding another book to the vast array of available literature on leadership, I decided to contribute to the discourse on relational leadership. My goal was to write a book that holistically examined relational leadership theory and connect strategies and practices extracted from diverse theoretical sources with real-life examples of how leaders apply relational leadership in real-world situations.

In today's volatile, uncertain, complex, and ambiguous (VUCA) marketplace, characterized by rapid technological advancements, shifting consumer behaviors, and unpredictable global events like the COVID-19 pandemic, the need for comprehensive theoretical and practical literature on relational leadership is more crucial than ever. *Leading Together: Unlocking Relational Leadership Mastery* is a practical guide to creating engaging, enduring, and performing organizational cultures. The relational practices highlighted in this book build on the archaic leader–follower, manager–subordinate concepts and focus on leadership as a shared social process, where leaders' and followers' effects on each other are equally valued. As traditional hierarchical models falter in the face of constant change, relational-based leadership offers a resilient framework for navigating uncertainty, creating positive, engaging cultures, and achieving organizational success.

While the content of this book is rooted in rigorous academic research on the relatively new concept of relational leadership, the book is dedicated to leader practitioners. The beauty of the relational leadership approach lies in its ability to transcend beyond the size and resources of organizations, bringing awareness to leaders who strive to enhance their personal and organizational effectiveness. This book elucidates the principles and practices of relational leadership, equipping leaders to thrive amidst VUCA marketplace challenges and cultivating organizational cultures where employees feel the company adds value rather than only expecting it from them. In return, this approach transforms employees into loyal and highly engaged stakeholders, enabling the organization to succeed.

CHAPTER 2

Evolution of Leadership

Ask a hundred people what leadership means, and you'll receive a hundred different answers. It's no wonder that hundreds of thousands of leadership books are written worldwide, with thousands more published each year. Leadership is a timeless concept that has captivated the minds of scholars, philosophers, and practitioners for centuries. From the heroic narratives of ancient mythology to the intricacies of modern organizational dynamics, the evolution of leadership reflects a rich tapestry of theories, paradigms, and practical applications. In this chapter, we embark on a journey through the evolution of leadership, tracing its origins from the seminal works of early philosophers to the contemporary insights of modern scholars. Our exploration will illuminate the dynamic nature of leadership and its enduring relevance in shaping the course of human endeavors. By understanding the historical evolution of the concept of leadership, our exploration will gain valuable insights into its transformative potential for leaders who strive to create engaging and thriving organizations amidst today's VUCA marketplace.

While the writings on leaders and leadership can be traced back to old Greek philosophers, the word leader, as we use it today, came to the English language in the 19th century. In his book *On Heroes, Hero-Worship, and the Heroic in Society*, Carlyle (1841) elaborated on how the history of the world is nothing but the biography of great men leading—the concept that gave birth to the Great Man theory. The story of King Arthur, one of the most prominent stories of European folklore, exemplifies the Great Man Theory. Anyone who knows this story understands that Arthur, chosen by a divine being, the Lady of the Lake, was destined to lead. By being the only man capable of pulling Excalibur from the stone, Arthur proved that he was born to lead.

Inspired mainly by male leaders in high positions, many writers supporting the Great Men theory (Cowley 1928; Galton 1869; Weber 1958) claimed that leadership qualities are inherently innate. This ideology laid the foundation for early trait theories, which sought to illustrate how specific personality traits, inherent since birth, could predict leadership success. Several notable works identified personality traits that differentiate individuals as leaders and followers. One of the pioneering works of trait theory is by Allport and Odbert (1936), which categorized traits as (a) cardinal—specific traits that differentiate individuals (e.g., Abraham Lincoln's honesty); (b) central—general characteristics of individuals, such as shyness or intelligence; and (c) secondary—traits that are sometimes related to attitude that often appears in specific situations (e.g., nervousness before public speaking). The list of the traits identified by Allport and Odbert (1936) was extensive. Later, Cattell (1965) grouped common characteristics from Allport and Odbert's (1936) initial list and consolidated the total into 171 traits. While the vigorous debate on personality traits continued for many decades, Eysenck (1992) was one of the first to make his approach quantifiable by narrowing the previously published extensive list of personality traits into three main areas: introversion/extroversion (a combination of sociability, impulsiveness, frivolity, and general activity), neuroticism (one's emotional stability, or lack thereof), and psychoticism (traits of dominance-leadership, dominance-submission, sensation seeking, and the lack of a superego). Believing that personality is primarily governed by biology, he claimed that personality traits exist in clusters and multiple characteristics may be concurrently active.

Critics of early trait theories claimed that Gordon Allport's theory is too broad, Cattell's theory is too complex, and Eysenck's theory is not empirically verifiable and, thus, too limited in scope (Kanodia and Sacher 2016). Subsequently, the Five-Factor Model emerged (Fiske 1949; Goldberg 1981; McCrae and Costa 1987; Norman 1967), describing essential individual traits as extraversion, agreeableness, conscientiousness, neuroticism, and openness. It is still considered one of the widely regarded theories, offering a middle ground among various early trait theories due to its effectiveness in providing a more comprehensive framework for understanding individual differences and variations in personality. However, one of the main criticisms of the Five-Factor trait theory is that it does not consider situational factors. For instance, if a leader exhibits a greater level of extraversion, creating a successful leadership outcome in one scenario, it does not mean that this trait can assist the leader in being effective in all other situations.

One of the early studies conducted by Terman on gifted children unveiled the dire limitations of the trait theory. Believing that intelligence quotient (IQ) was a predictor of the likelihood of one's future success, Terman worked closely with California's elementary and high schools to conduct IQ tests on the student population in the state. Through a series of tests, Terman ultimately identified 1470 children whose IQs averaged between 140 and 200 (as cited in Gladwell 2008). Convinced that these children would be future national leaders, Terman meticulously followed their lives and methodically documented every success in their professional careers in his *Genetic Studies of Genius* research. Unfortunately, "by the time the Termites reached adulthood, Terman's error was plain to see" (Gladwell 2008, 89). While many of these children became productive members of society, most had careers that "could only be considered ordinary, and a surprising number ended up with careers that even Terman considered failures" (Gladwell 2008, 89). None of them emerged as nationally known figures. Ironically, Terman rejected two students from his study for not having a high enough IQ, who later became Nobel laureates (as cited in Gladwell 2008). Terman's study demonstrated that personality traits alone do not determine leadership effectiveness or predict who can lead.

So, if personality traits do not predict leadership effectiveness, then what does? Convinced by the limitation of trait theories, Stogdill (1948) claimed that leadership occurs between individuals in a social context, where individuals in leadership roles and their followers equally influence each other. He believed that the leader who is effective in one situation may not be able to successfully lead in another. For instance, a highly extrovert leader who may be well-suited to lead a particular sales organization may not be the optimal choice to lead a team of engineers in another organization focusing on research and development. Stogdill's

(1948) comments led researchers to shift the focus from personality traits as leadership predictors to leaders' behaviors and the situations in which leadership occurs, thus giving rise to behavioral leadership theories.

One of the early studies on behavioral leadership was conducted in the 1940s by Ohio State University. Based on numerous employee interviews, the Ohio State University research narrowed leadership behaviors into two categories: initiating structure behavior and consideration behavior. Leaders initiate structure behavior, clearly define leader–subordinate roles and expectations, and establish transparent processes and communication lines to ensure followers perform specific tasks according to the plan. On the other hand, leaders engaged in consideration behavior are concerned for their subordinate's welfare and attempt to create a trust-based, friendly work environment. The study also showed that these two behavioral dimensions are not mutually exclusive, and scoring low in one does not automatically mean a leader would score high in another. The study found that leaders rated high in both dimensions were likelier to achieve high employee engagement and performance. However, what was intriguing was that a high-high rating did not always render positive consequences. In some cases, a high rating in the initiating structure behavior dimension resulted in higher absenteeism and employee turnover levels. Alternatively, a high rating in the consideration behavior resulted in lower performance evaluation scores from the leaders' managers. While the study suggested that a high-high rating generally resulted in positive outcomes, sufficient evidence indicated that situational factors equally mattered.

As a result, several contingency models emerged through research in the late 1900s (Fiedler 1964; Hersey and Blanchard 1969; House 1996). Focusing on the importance of a leader's personality and the unique situation surrounding the leader, Fiedler (1964) outlined two styles of leadership: task-motivated, referring to task accomplishment, and relationship-motivated, referring to interpersonal relationships. Fiedler's (1964) Least Preferred Co-Worker metric demonstrated a leadership scoring scale, where leaders are categorized as relationship or task-motivated depending on how high or low they score. The Path-Goal theory, later reformulated by House (1996), focused on how different leadership behaviors, such as directive, supportive, achieve-ment-oriented, and participative, can assist followers in accomplishing their goals. The type of style is contingent on the unique task in which followers are engaged. On the other hand, Hersey and Blanchard's (1969) model focused on the maturity level of subordinates, which then triggers the preferred style of leaders in each situation.

While contingency theories remain popular today and help account for unique leadership situations where leader–follower exchanges occur, they fail to explain how leaders adapt and change their behaviors or styles (Gill 2011). For example, consider a contingency theory applied in an organization where a leader must navigate routine operations and sudden emergencies. While the theory may provide insights into which leadership characteristic is more effective in such situations, it may not fully elucidate how leaders transition between styles or adapt their behavior to address evolving challenges in real time. Thus, despite its popularity, contingency theories appear vastly limiting in predicting leadership success.

More recent theoretical developments in leadership theory, such as Social Constructivism, view trait-based, behavior-based, and contin-gency-based models as significantly limiting, focusing on individual decision makers only. The fundamental assumption of the trait-based theories is that certain traits can predict leadership success. The underlying assumption of situational theories is that not only is the correct analysis of a particular situation possible, but it can also trigger a particular leadership response toward a successful outcome. Finally, the primary assumption of contingency theories is that it is possible to correctly identify the leadership and situational characteristics that could lead toward the successful adaptation of the two (Billsberry 2009). Grint (2005) called these assumptions naïve and argued that they underestimate the extent to which the context or a particular situation is actively created. He claimed that individual leaders are not independ-ent agents, freely able to manipulate the world around them. Instead, Grint contemplated that they are part of the "social construction of the context that both legitimates a particular form of action and constitutes the world in the process" (Gring 2005, 1471).

Contrary to the Great Man Theory we highlighted at the beginning of this chapter, modern leadership paradigms depict leaders not only as architects of organizational cultures but also as products of the influence wielded by the people within the organization. While this revelation may not be groundbreaking, it should serve as a poignant reminder of humility for leaders. And when we say humility, we're not talking about the false modesty often seen in many contemporary leaders—a trait CS Lewis famously compared to 99 percent arrogance. Instead, we refer to a deep-seated, authentic humility that recognizes the value of others in the organization settings, which lays the groundwork for this book. This insight emphasizes that effective leadership transcends individual actions, advocating for a collaborative approach to crafting a relational world where leaders and followers coalesce to create environments where the organization and its people can thrive together.

CHAPTER 3

The Paradigm Shift

No story better illustrates the concept of a paradigm shift than the tale of U.S. automakers, capturing their rise, fall, and eventual historic rebound. This narrative vividly demonstrates how a once-dominant industry lost its global leadership by failing to recognize emerging trends and by not questioning its deep-rooted beliefs about how success is achieved in a changing socioeconomic climate. Yet, through adapting to new realities, embracing innovation, and undergoing a strategic transformation, the industry fundamentally changed its thinking and methodologies, ultimately reclaiming its position in the global market.

On June 16, 1903, Henry Ford established the Ford Motor Company with a dream to revolutionize the mass-producing assembly line for automobiles. Shortly after its inception, the company assembled its first Ford Model A from a tiny manufacturing workshop in Detroit, Michigan. It quickly outgrew the original facility, and on April 10, 1904, Ford purchased a piece of land on Piquette Avenue in Detroit to build a much larger factory. And the rest is history.

In the same year Ford Motor Company opened its doors, William Durant started General Motors, doubling its sales force within the first year to keep up with the demand. It rapidly acquired 20 different automobile companies, becoming one of the leading automobile manufacturing companies in the United States along with Ford. Two decades after General Motors opened for business, Chrysler was born. Competing with its U.S. counterparts by introducing multiple impressive and widely popular vehicle models such as Plymouth, DeSoto, and Dodge, it quickly joined the top echelon of automakers along with Ford and General Motors. For the next 50 years, Ford, General Motors, and Chrysler, later dubbed the Big Three, dominated the United States and global auto manufacturing. Their grip on the industry was so tight that everyone thought these titans were an immutable part of the industry, destined to reign forever in the world of automobiles.

However, fast forward another 50 years, the automobile industry landscape looked drastically different. Not only had the Big Three lost their global leadership position, but they had also ceded over 40 percent of the U.S. market share to foreign automakers, particularly the Japanese. General Motors' share alone of the U.S. market plummeted nearly threefold from its peak of 50.7 percent in 1962 to 17 percent in the 2000s (*Top Vehicle Manufacturers in the U.S. Markets, 1961–2016,* 2020).

Compared to their American counterparts, the trajectory of Japanese automakers followed a strikingly different path. In the 1950s, Japanese automakers slowly began enhancing their manufacturing capabilities. Throughout the 1950s, even after the government's support to restrict car imports in the country, enabling local auto companies to expand, the Japanese car market remained localized and relatively insignificant for the global competition to pay much attention to. However, in the 1960s, Japanese automakers started to gain significant traction in European and U.S. markets by focusing on operational innovations and cost efficiencies. By the 1970s, Japan exported over one million cars annually, primarily to the United States. The 1973 oil crisis further propelled the popularity of Japanese cars in the United States. By 2008, Japan had surpassed the United States as the global leader in car manufacturing (Klier 2009).

So, what caused such an extraordinary shift in the automobile industry? Among many factors that contributed to such a dramatic shift, a primary factor that led the U.S. automakers to lose a significant market share was their failure to recognize and adapt to evolving consumer preferences. While the U.S. car manufacturers focused on internal competition for automobile designs, believing that cars should reflect one's status symbol and prioritizing style over cost and quality, they overlooked the growing demand for smaller, more comfortable, fuel-efficient, and affordable vehicles. Even when compact and subcompact vehicle sales accounted for 60 percent of the total U.S. market, Detroit automakers dismissed competitor offerings as inferior, resentfully attributing their lower prices to cheap labor resources overseas. This perspective was epitomized by General Motors, which viewed the small car market as a passing trend, calling it "an unpleasant aberration that would vanish" (Smith 1987, 3). Today, we know all too well that many years later, this decision became one they deeply regretted, as American auto manufacturers found themselves desperately racing to catch up to their Japanese counterparts.

Indeed, hindsight is often 20–20, and overlooking market indicators and missing socioeconomic trends are not exclusive to Detroit automakers. Nevertheless, what adds to the tragedy in this historic example is that long before the Big Three lost a substantial market share to their competition, they had the opportunity to visit Japanese factories and witness their operations firsthand. Despite this chance, they failed to recognize that the success of Japanese car manufacturers might be due to factors beyond just access to "cheap" labor. In "The Fifth Discipline," Senge (1990), an American systems theorist, recounts speaking with Detroit executives following their visit to Japan several years earlier. He was taken aback to learn the Detroit executives' claims that the Japanese showcased them fake auto plants. One senior manager justified this claim by saying: "There were no inventories in any of the plants. I've been in manufacturing operations for almost thirty years, and I can tell you those were not real plants" (as cited in Senge 1990). Mark Twain once said: "It ain't what you don't know that gets you into trouble; It's what you know for sure that just ain't so." In the minds of Detroit auto executives, the operational methods of U.S. plants were perceived as the key to sustained success, especially considering their history of significant achievements over decades. The U.S. automakers were accustomed to auto plants in Detroit filled with excess inventory and spare parts. Subsequently, when they didn't observe a similar environment during their visit to Japanese auto factories, they concluded that Japanese factories must have been fake. Years later, Detroit auto executives had to drastically shift their perspectives when they discovered that the Japanese were employing a "Just-in-time" inventory management system, which allowed them to operate their factories without excess inventory, resulting in more cost-effective automotive production. Consequently, Detroit automakers experienced a paradigm shift.

From a learning standpoint, it's crucial to note that the mistake of the Detroit automakers wasn't due to their stubbornness, unwillingness, or inability to learn and succeed. In fact, the U.S. auto industry has demonstrated a significant revitalization in the last decade primarily due to its commitment to quality, innovative production, and management techniques. Ford alone reported record profits of $21.69 billion in 2021, $23.66 billion in 2022, and $25.64 billion in 2023 (Ford Motor Gross Profit 2010–2023 n.d.). Instead, the historical blunder of Detroit executives stemmed from a common error experienced by individuals and organizations everywhere—a concept Senge (1990) dubbed mental models. He defines mental models as a phenomenon where "new insights fail to get put into practice because they conflict with deeply held internal images of how the world works, images that limit us to familiar ways of thinking and acting" (p. 163). Leaders who remain unaware of their mental models do not seek to examine them. Subsequently, unexamined mental models remain unchanged, eventually leading to increasingly faulty decision-making and devastating results for their organizations.

So, how do leaders become aware of their mental models? A famous dictum attributed to Socrates during his trial of impiety may offer a historical context for the answer: "The unexamined life is not worth living." In a more contemporary era, Donald Schon, an MIT professor and one of the first scholars to write about exploring experience and reflection, calls for the importance of being reflective practitioners. Schon (1983) wrote that while many adults seem to stop active learning as soon as they leave universities, those who practice being lifelong learners can become true reflective practitioners and distinguish themselves as outstanding professionals.

However, it is imperative to note that being a reflective practitioner goes beyond continuous formal or informal education. It is often ironic to read how leaders boast about being lifelong learners, highlighting their engagement in various educational programs, certificates, degrees, and the consumption of academic and nonacademic texts. Yet, whether accidentally or purposefully, some leaders ignore a simple and arguably one of the most effective methods for learning—feedback. Receiving feedback, especially from those individuals with whom a leader does not feel comfortable or agree, is one of the most potent tools for self-examination and lifelong learning. Let's explore the following question if you believe this is an overgeneralization or a misleading assumption. Why don't leaders conduct exit interviews with departing employees themselves instead of leaving this task to human resources departments? And I don't mean the cursory conversation with the departing employee that typically ends in superficial comments, but rather direct and humble inquiry for personal feedback for improvement. While legal and risk management reasons might be cited, the fact remains that not a single leader I have encountered at several Fortune 500 companies has taken the time to sit down directly with a departing employee to seek candid feedback about their leadership. What a missed opportunity!

Directly conducting exit interviews could provide leaders with honest, unbiased feedback and the chance to learn what the leader can do better. Such firsthand information could reveal hidden issues, offer insights into leadership challenges and workplace culture, and highlight areas for improvement. By neglecting this opportunity, leaders miss out on valuable lessons that could enhance their leadership effectiveness and ongoing personal development.

This is the reason Senge (1990) advocates for implementing ongoing feedback loops—a reciprocal flow of influence that leaders can master by creating an environment of "reciprocal inquiry" (p. 184). He contends that everyone in the organization, especially leaders, should make their thinking "explicit and subject to public examination" (p. 184). Senge (1990) argues that when leaders fail to build effective relationships with stakeholders and create an environment where candid feedback is freely exchanged, they risk developing "unexamined mental models" (p. 166), which can lead to detrimental outcomes for both the leaders and the organizations they lead.

Danish author Hans Christian Andersen felicitously depicted this concept in his literary folktale, *The Emperor's New Clothes*, where a vein emperor gets exposed in front of his subjects because no one dares to offer him honest feedback. This anecdotal illustration depicts two con men pretending to be weavers, promising to create magnificent new clothes for the emperor while assuring him that the clothes would be invisible to those who are stupid or incompetent. In actuality, the weavers create no clothes at all. When the emperor parades in front of his ministers and advisors wearing invisible garments, no one dares to share that he is completely exposed, fearing that they will be considered stupid and incompetent. Subsequently, the emperor parades naked in front of the whole city, and townsfolk uncomfortably go along with the pretense, fearing to appear stupid. When a child starts laughing at the emperor, pointing out that he is entirely naked, the townspeople finally understand the truth. Still, the emperor, set in his beliefs, continues to parade completely naked.

Unfortunately, the metaphorical message described in this humorous story is very much present in many large corporations and small businesses today. Granted, numerous factors can create negative business environments where trust is low between leaders and followers, preventing employees from providing honest, helpful feedback. However, I remain resolute that it is often the leaders' inability or unwillingness to build close, mutually beneficial relationships with stakeholders throughout the organization that prevents them from receiving ongoing candid feedback, becoming a critical factor in forming negative organizational cultures. Suppose the reader is skeptical about such an assumption. In that case, once again, I ask the question— why is there so much outcry from employees about negative leaders, toxic organizational cultures, disengagement, and lack of psychological safety in the workplace? Learning from the dire lessons of Detroit automakers, is it time we question our unexamined mental models and perhaps experience a paradigm shift?

To create an organizational culture where feedback is welcomed, expected, and freely given by all stakeholders, Senge (1990) advocates for leaders to foster the creation of learning organizations where new patterns of thinking are nurtured, and leaders and followers are continually learning to see the big picture together. Leaders who create such relational cultures are rewarded by their followers transforming into highly engaged and loyal evangelists for the leader and the leader's cause (Antonakis 2012; Bass 1985, 1999). Such relational cultures serve as the antidote to the negative employee–employer and organization––employee trends in today's VUCA marketplace. These are the very concepts that establish the context for the relational leadership model we will explore in the next chapter.

CHAPTER 4

What Is Relational Leadership?

In its simplest form, relational leadership is a leadership practice that emphasizes a collective effort to cultivate a relational environment in which leaders, followers, and their respective organizations flourish. This type of collective win-win-win approach enables the creation of a high-quality workplace environment, which is the key focus of the relational leadership model. A quality workplace environment, as defined in this book, is characterized by an organizational culture where individual differences are genuinely nurtured, information is not suppressed or spun but instead openly shared, where employees feel the company adds value to them instead of always expecting it from them, and where the leaders and followers equally dedicate the best versions of themselves to each other and their organizations' shared goals (Goffee and Jones 2013; Katz and Miller 2014; Tan 2019).

While the concept of relationship-oriented leadership has been examined in various scholarly writings (Brower et al. 2000; Graen and Uhl-Bien 1995; Murrell 1997; Uhl-Bien 2006), the term relational leadership is relatively new. Upon closer examination of the literature on this subject, it became evident that the term "relational" carries distinct interpretations across researchers approaching this concept from diverse theoretical perspectives (Dachler and Hosking 1995a; Dansereau et al. 1975; Graen and Uhl-Bien 1995; Hollander 1992; Uhl-Bien 2006). Many theorists focus on exploring relationship-oriented behaviors from an individual standpoint, either from the leader's or follower's perspective (Bass 1985; Brower et al. 2000; Burns 1978; Dansereau et al. 1975; Drath 1990; Graen 2016; Graen and Uhl-Bien 1995; Hollander 1992). While these writings suggest that relationship-focused exchanges between leaders and followers create open, supportive, trust-based working environments that "encourage people to leave their comfort zones and explore how their purpose might be better met at work" (Dewar et al. 2020, 3), they are constrained by the fact that such relational environments primarily emanate from one individual, typically the leader. Relational leadership theory builds on these archaic leader–follower, manager–subordinate relationships and focuses on the "relational processes by which leadership is produced and enabled" (Uhl-Bien 2006, 667). A significant number of scholarly writings (Dachler and Hosking 1995a; Graen and Uhl-Bien 1995; Hosking 1988; Hosking and Pluut 2010; Murrell 1997; Uhl-Bien 2006) suggest the evolution of the term relational leadership toward a view of "leadership and organization as human social constructions that emanate from the rich connections and interdependencies of organizations and their members" (Uhl-Bien 2006, 655). In other words, these scholars promote the idea that it's not one leader or even a group of leaders but the dynamic relationships and interactions among all stakeholders that fundamentally shape leadership and organizations.

More recent scholarly contributions advancing relational leadership theory are credited to Mary Uhl-Bien (2006), who delineates two distinct perspectives within the relational leadership framework: entity and relational perspectives. While subsequent chapters delve deeper into these viewpoints, it's essential to understand their foundational distinctions.

The *entity* perspective is considered more traditional, focusing on individual leaders and followers, their characteristics, and how they build mutually beneficial work environments through individual actions. This approach focuses on leadership through individual "perceptions, intentions, behaviors, personalities, expectations, and evaluations relative to their relationships with one other" (Uhl-Bien 2006, 655). Many relationship-oriented behavior-based leadership theories, such as Servant, Transformational, Charismatic, Situational leadership, and Leader–Member Exchange (LMX) theories, to name a few, fit well within this perspective. While some of these theories incorporate some components of collective leadership—leaders and followers creating leadership cultures together—the primary focus remains on leaders as individuals and their actions to ignite relational dynamics.

In contrast to the entity approach, the *relational* perspective shifts the focus toward the process of relational leadership creation, where leaders and followers are collectively responsible for creating a quality workplace environment. Uhl-Bien (2006) contends that in the relational perspective model, "leadership is not concentrated within certain individuals but is distributed throughout the social field" (p. 662). Contrary to many traditional leadership theories, where the leader is a central figure in creating a trust-based, cohesive organizational environment, the relational perspective promotes the creation of such relationship-based environments as a collective mission of all individuals involved in the process.

To establish the epistemological context for relational theory, it is crucial to avoid viewing the two relational leadership perspectives in isolation or favoring one approach over the other. Uhl-Bien (2006) suggests that while the implications for the research and practice of the entity and relational perspectives are different, relational leadership theory draws from both viewpoints. Examining these two perspectives holistically will thoroughly explore how leaders and followers interact to create a relational environment and how organizations benefit from these dynamics.

Utilizing Uhl-Bien's (2006) relational leadership theory as a theoretical framework, this book examines various leadership models from both entity and relational perspectives in the forthcoming chapters. While the goal is to explore how real-life leaders practice relational leadership, highlighted in Chapters 9 and 10, we must first obtain a comprehensive understanding of the holistic view of the theoretical model. Such an exploratory journey will help our readers, as reflective practitioners, to better recognize how relational leaders embody the principles of relational leadership to foster high-quality workplace environments amidst today's VUCA marketplace challenges.

CHAPTER 5

The Entity Perspective

This chapter provides an in-depth exploration of the entity perspective within relational leadership theory. Several supporting leadership theories are highlighted to give the reader a clear understanding of how various leadership theories, often covered in multiple corporate leadership development programs, fit within this perspective. Additionally, the chapter highlights the drawbacks of viewing and practicing leadership solely consistent with the entity perspective and sets the stage for exploring the relational perspective.

As mentioned earlier, the entity perspective focuses on the individual characteristics of leaders and followers and their perceptions, behaviors, and interactions (Uhl-Bien 2006). As a traditional view, the entity perspective incorporates various models that explore leadership from the standpoint of "individuals as independent, discrete entities" (Uhl-Bien 2006, 655). Dachler and Hosking (1995a) called the entity perspective possessive individualism, explaining that theories that fit within this construct typically emphasize individuals as entities, where leaders "are understood to possess certain characteristics on the basis of which they carry out their leadership functions" (p. 7). The following sections delve into the entity perspective of relational leadership theory by exploring various theories, including leader–member exchange (LMX), leader–member, member–member exchange (LMX-MMX), Hollander's relational theory, transformational leadership, charismatic leadership, servant leadership, individual and collective self-concepts, social networks, self-efficacy, and emotional intelligence (EI). Let's explore these models one by one.

LMX Theory

One of the most prominent relationship-based approaches is the LMX theory. Before the LMX theory, researchers treated leadership as something leaders did toward all their followers. Dansereau et al. (1975) challenged the existing models by pointing out two erroneous assumptions that these theories predominantly hold. The first assumption is that the followers in the same organizational unit under one leader are "sufficiently homogeneous on the relevant dimensions (e.g., perceptions, interpretations, and reactions) and that they can be considered as a single entity" (Dansereau et al. 1975, 47). The second assumption is that leaders behave in essentially the same manner toward all followers. Contrary to these assumptions, LMX theory focuses on the relationship between a leader and a follower contained in a dyad. This approach allows for the case where "each of the vertical dyadic relationships contained within a unit are radically different" (p. 47).

The central concept of the LMX theory is that leadership occurs when leaders and followers develop effective relationships that result in incremental influence. As a result, they gain access to the many benefits these relationships bring. LMX theory describes how effective leadership relationships develop among dyad partners, such as leaders and team members or peers, to generate bases of leadership influence (Graen 2016; Uhl-Bien 2006). Early LMX theory focused on two general types of relationships: in-groups and out-groups. Followers become a part of the in-group or the out-group based on how well they work with the leader and how well the leader works with them (Dansereau et al. 1975). In-group followers enjoy increased job latitude and greater confidence from leaders, often resulting in reciprocation from in-group followers, who assume "greater responsibility and commitment to the success of the organization" (Lunenburg 2010, 2). Relationships with out-group members are typically governed "within the narrow limits of their formal employment contract" (p. 2). Leaders who understand the significance of LMX recognize that they need to avoid creating out-groups wherever possible and maximize the size of the in-group. Research shows that high-quality LMX produces less employee turnover, more significant organizational commitment, better job attitudes, more attention and support from the leader, and greater engagement from employees (Beverly 2016; Gajendran and Aparna 2012; Graen 2016; Lunenburg 2010; Power 2013).

LMX-MMX Sharing Network Theory

More recent research has moved beyond the dyadic relationships and has begun to explore the interrelationships between and among leaders and followers (Graen 2016). Graen (2016) offered a transformation of LMX theory to the new LMX-MMX theory of sharing network leadership and proposed that leadership moves beyond the limiting supervisor–follower relationship to outside formal reporting structures. He called this construct a "leadership sharing process" (Graen 2016, 26). Graen (2016) argued that such a leadership sharing process is different from "dumping unwanted tasks, formal or informal delegation, and getting someone to do your pseudo leadership sharing" (p. 26). The LMX-MMX model maintains that leaders and followers share risks and rewards collectively and equitably, which involves a higher level of trust, mutual respect, and commitment from the parties involved to maintain its development (Graen 2016).

Graen (2016) drew differences between LMX-MMX and other leadership models by arguing that LMX-MMX team leaders prefer followers with clearly defined self-concepts who want to make helpful suggestions for improvements. In contrast, charismatic leaders seek followers with more ambiguous self-concepts, who prefer leaders to give directions. Charismatic leaders attempt to persuade followers to embrace change and achieve transformation with strong engagement and increase the intrinsic value of followers to accomplish the set vision (Fiol et al. 1999). To develop a quality leadership sharing culture, Graen (2016) suggested that leaders assess the characteristics of their team members in terms of these two leadership styles. If the employees prefer to contribute to creating the leadership culture, they are predisposed to LMX leadership sharing. In contrast, they are predisposed to charismatic leadership if they like to be told what to do and avoid the responsibility of enriched roles (Graen 2016).

Hollander's Relational Theory

Hollander provided yet another prominent relationship-based approach to leadership. The essential points of his model are: (a) leadership is a process of establishing and influencing relationships, (b) the leader is one among other participants in the relationship-building process, and (c) certain interactions occur between leaders and followers which Hollander calls transactions exchanges (Hollander 1992; Uhl-Bien 2006). Hollander (2010) argued that followers have certain expectations of the benefits their leaders will provide. These benefits are essential to leader–follower interdependence, and leaders use them to reward followers who support the leader (Hollander 1992, 2010). Furthermore, Hollander (1992, 2010) argued that leaders are given a certain latitude in credit-building. He contended that this process is a function of the followers' perceptions of the leader's competency and relatability, which creates follower trust and loyalty in the leader. To build on Hollander's (1992) argument, it is noteworthy that self-absorbed leaders often fail to build trust and loyalty with their employees (McCall et al. 1988). David Lee Roth's famous quote, an ounce of image is worth a pound of performance, holds true here. In some cases, employee perceptions of their leaders may obscure the realities of the leader's performance, at least in the short term (McCall et al. 1988). Hollander (1992) contended that leaders who are consumed with managing their self-image may become detached from their followers and "cease to be concerned about how their actions will be perceived by and affect followers and their mutual activities" (p. 72). Subsequently, relationships between leaders and followers diminish in strength and value.

McCall et al. (1988), who extensively worked on how successful executives develop on the job, conducted a study of 400 up-and-coming executives. They found that those executives failing to reach their expected potential tended to show inconsiderate behaviors toward others. McCall et al. (1988) claimed that only rich human connections and relationships move managers through the learning process and advance them to their full potential.

Consistent with the entity perspective, Hollander (1992) focused on the relational process from the standpoint of the individual. However, he claimed, "Leaders do command greater attention and influence, but followers can affect and even constrain leaders' activity in more than passive ways" (Hollander 1992, 71). By stating the above, he transitioned the focus from leaders, their functions, traits, and behaviors to "qualities and responsiveness of followers, with their needs, expectations, and perceptions" (p. 71). According to Hollander (1992), positive qualities sought in good leaders, such as honesty, dependability, and trustworthiness, are also included among the attributes of good followers. While certain traits in leaders, such as drive, honesty and integrity, self-confidence, and cognitive ability, matter (Kirkpatrick and Locke 1991), Hollander (1992) claimed that these traits are more important within the context of their fit with the "followers' attributions about leaders and if they elicit a response, affirmative or otherwise, from followers" (p. 71).

One criticism of Hollander's (1992) theory is that leaders may attract only a particular type of followers that fits within their leadership style. For example, authoritarian leaders may attract followers who want to appease the leader and may be uncomfortable speaking their minds freely. Therefore, looking at the relational component of the leader–follower dynamic through Hollander's lens presents particular challenges for leaders with an authoritarian leadership style. To create effective work environments, leaders should strive to stimulate honest, constructive dissent, and the failure to do so may have devastating consequences for leaders and the organizations they serve (Roberto 2005).

Transformational Leadership

Burns's (1978) transformational leadership theory can also be considered another traditional relational leadership approach, as it roots itself in relational interdependencies between leaders and followers. Even though he first introduced the transformational leadership theory in his research on political leaders, it is widely used across multiple disciplines. Transformational leadership is a process in which leaders and followers help each other to advance to a higher-level motivation and morality. Burns (1978) claimed, "Leadership is relational, collective, and purposeful" (p. 12). He delineated the concept of leadership from leaders having power over subordinates, claiming, "We must see power—and leadership—as not a thing but as relationships" (p. 11). This reciprocal benefit sharing through leader–follower exchanges is particularly noteworthy in the transformational leadership theory within the context of the relational approach.

Burns (1978) contended that not all human influences are necessarily coercive and exploitative, and "most powerful influences consist of deeply human relationships in which two or more persons engage with one another" (p. 11). Still, he distinguishes between transformational and transactional leadership by arguing that these concepts are mutually exclusive. According to Burns (1978), transformational leaders uplift morale and motivation in their followers, and through this process, "both leader and follower are raised to higher levels of motivation and morality" (p. 20). On the other hand, transactional leaders cater to their followers' immediate self-interest (Bass 1999). Despite the lower perceived value of transactional leadership, it is noteworthy that all leader–follow exchanges have a transactional component (Bass 1985, 1999; Hollander 1992). For example, at the heart of every employment relationship lies a transaction: An employer offers a compensation package to an employee in exchange for the performance of specific services, while the employee expects compensation for the services rendered.

Bass (1985), who built his work on Burns's (1978) theory, argued that while transactional and transformational leadership are separate, they are also complementary concepts coexisting on a single leadership continuum. He further claimed that the best leaders are transformational and transactional in style (Bass 1985, 1999; Bass and Riggio 2006). An example would be an employee who provides services to an employer in exchange for compensation (transactional component) while also developing a close, trust-based relationship with their leader and going above and beyond what's expected to support the leader and the organization (transformational component).

While transactional leadership emphasizes the exchange between leaders and followers, transformational leadership raises this dynamic to the next level (Bass 1985; Burns 1978). Transformational leaders inspire followers to commit to an organization's shared vision and goals and "motivate others to do more than they originally intended and often even more than they thought possible" (Bass and Riggio 2006, 4). These leaders empower their employees by paying attention to their individual needs and personal development while helping them reach their leadership potential (Bass and Riggio 2006).

Because "transformational leaders can be directive or participative, authoritarian or democratic" (Bass 1999, 13), Bass (1999) offered a new term, pseudotransformational leadership, to separate from the transformational concept those leaders who are self-consumed, exploitive, and power-oriented, with warped moral values (Bass and Riggio 2006). Examples of such leaders are Hitler, Stalin, and Pinochet, to name a few. Pseudotransformational leaders focus on their interests rather than followers (Bass and Steidlmeier 1999); therefore, this research excludes pseudotransformational leadership from the relational leadership construct.

Components of Transformational Leadership

Transformational leadership motivates followers to surpass expectations by focusing on idealized influence, inspirational motivation, intellectual stimulation, and individualized consideration (Bass 1985). Idealized influence, which is also referred to as charisma and inspirational leadership, is displayed when the leader "envisions a desirable future, articulates how it can be reached, sets an example to be followed, sets high standards of performance, and shows determination and confidence" (Bass 1999, 11). Such leaders engage followers to share their vision and dedicate themselves to the cause (Bass 1999). Leaders display intellectual stimulation when helping followers become more creative to support the cause. Last, leaders display individualized consideration by paying attention to the followers' developmental needs and emotional support. Followers often get rewarded by various opportunities that help them realize their potential as leaders.

The critics of transformational leadership theory argue that it lacks conceptual clarity because it covers a wide range of leadership characteristics, such as charisma, vision creation, and employee motivation through tapping into their emotional and intellectual needs, to name a few (Tracey and Hinkin 1998). Additionally, there is skepticism in research about whether the transformational leadership approach creates long-term change in individuals and organizations (Bass 1999; Bryman 1993). Yukl (1999) argued that similar to early leadership theories that focused on traits of leaders, transformational leadership theory reflects an implicit assumption of the "heroic leadership" (p. 292) stereotype, which may be finite and inadequate in building quality workplace environments at the workplace.

Relational Leadership Through Service Versus Charisma

Leadership studies have recently moved away from a strong focus on transformational and charismatic leadership approaches toward a stronger emphasis on a shared, relational, and global perspective, where leader–follower interactions and relation-building are focal points (Avolio et al. 2009; Graham 1991). While transformational and charismatic leadership models focus on transcendent and far-reaching ideas and goals (Antonakis 2012), servant leadership incorporates social responsibility (Avolio et al. 2009; Graham 1991), which may be of particular relevance in today's era (Van Dierendonck 2011). While charismatic and transformational models approach leadership from the leader's perspective, servant leadership's focal point is the followers' well-being (Antonakis 2012; Avolio et al. 2009; Bass 1985, 1999; Bass and Riggio 2006; House 1976; Van Dierendonck 2011). Despite their fundamental differences, these models concentrate on the individual interactions between leaders and followers and, therefore, are part of the traditional perspective of the relational leadership theory.

Servant Leadership

Greenleaf's (1977) servant leadership theory is strongly present in this relatively new field of positive organizational behavior that focuses on employees and social responsibility (Van Dierendonck 2011). It fits well within the relational leadership perspective and emphasizes the leader's focus on the followers, development, empowerment, and well-being.

Greenleaf (1977) credited his work in servant leadership theory to a novel by Hesse (1956), *The Journey to the East*. Hesse (1956) told the story of a group of men on a mystical journey accompanied by a servant named Leo, who performs menial chores and provides spiritual encouragement to the group. After Leo suddenly disappears, the group falls into disarray and abandons the journey. Later, one of the journeymen is asked to appear before the high throne to be judged by the league officials who sponsored the journey. At that moment, he identifies Leo as the titled leader of the league. Hesse (1956) was inspired by this novel and focused his work on Leo being primarily a servant, even though he was also a leader.

According to Greenleaf (1977), "The great leader is seen as servant first, and that simple fact is the key to his greatness" (p. 27). He contended that the concept of servant-first versus leader-first is on the opposite side of the spectrum of leadership. Even though both types aspire to lead, the servant-first leader puts the follower's needs as the highest priority above all (Greenleaf 1977). He offered additional qualifications for the definition of servant leadership by asking if those who are served grow as leaders and if they become "healthier, wiser, freer, more autonomous, more likely themselves to become servants" (Greenleaf 1977, 27). Greenleaf (1977) also questioned servant leadership's impact on society and those who are least privileged. He asked, "Will they benefit, or, at least, not be further deprived?" (p. 27).

Greenleaf (1977) argued that testing servant leadership's effectiveness is difficult. Because "servant leaders exhibit love in numerous ways" (Patterson 2003, 3), there is simply a multitude of variables to identify and measure (Avolio et al. 2009). Despite Greenleaf (1977) introducing the theory more than 40 years ago, followed by numerous researchers offering theoretical models, there is still no consensus about a definition and theoretical framework of servant leadership (Van Dierendonck 2011).

One servant leadership model, among many, is by Coetzer et al. (2017), who offered eight characteristics of a servant leader:

- Authenticity—leaders showing their true identity
- Humility—leaders being modest with high self-awareness
- Compassion—leaders caring for others
- Accountability—leaders being accountable and transparent;
- Courage—leaders standing up for what is morally right;
- Altruism—leaders being selfless and focused on others;
- Integrity—leaders being honest, fair, and ethical
- Listening—leaders listen actively and respectfully

Unfortunately, while most writings on servant leadership and its characteristics are aspirational, focusing on what servant leadership should ideally be, there is little agreement among researchers on the characteristics and normative principles of the servant leadership model (Block 2006; Coetzer et al. 2017; Patterson 2003; Russell and Stone 2002; Spears 2010; Van Dierendonck 2011). Consequently, this lack of consensus presents a significant challenge for this theoretical model to be considered comprehensive and inclusive.

Charismatic Leadership

While the theory of charismatic leadership is widely associated with Weber (1947), Aristotle wrote in *Rhetoric* that a leader must gain the followers' confidence by using creative rhetorical means to rouse followers' emotions, provide a moral direction, and use reasoning. In this context, the concept of charismatic leadership can be dated back to the days of Aristotle (Antonakis 2012). Weber (1947) suggested three types of authority: the traditional, the rational-legal, and the charismatic. The first two concepts of authority are legitimated by the sanctity of tradition (traditional authority) and legal order (rational-legal; Weber 1947). Arguably, the most distinctive type of authority rests upon charisma. Weber (1947) argued that charismatic leaders possess an extraordinary gift, which enables leaders to have "profound and extraordinary effects on followers" (House 1976, 4). House (1976) contended that this gift is a complex set of behaviors from the leader, characteristics of the followers, and situational factors surrounding specific interactions.

To identify better charisma or charismatic leaders, Tucker (1968) and House (1976) first proposed defining it regarding its effects on followers. House (1976) suggested that researchers can identify charismatic leadership only after impacting others. He offered several potential effects charismatic leaders have on followers:

> Followers trust in the correctness of the leader's beliefs, the similarity of followers' beliefs to those of the leader, unquestioning acceptance of the leader, affection for the leader, willing obedience to the leader, identification with and emulation of the leader, emotional involvement of the follower in the mission, heightened goals of the follower, and the feeling on the part of followers that they will be able to accomplish or contribute to the accomplishment of the mission (House 1976, 7).

However, Tucker (1968) cautioned not to confuse charisma with power because "power is a source of phenomena that resembles the effects of charisma without actually being such" (p. 740). He pointed out the example of Stalin in 1940s Russia and claimed that his people did not worship Stalin in the way foreign visitors perceived based on what they saw and heard from his followers when Stalin was in power. Therefore, Tucker (1968) suggested that examining leaders' impact on their followers would be more applicable before the leader achieves office and becomes politically powerful. Thus, the "pre-power stage of a leader's career is of critical significance" (Tucker 1968, 740).

Charismatic leadership is often attributed to three personal characteristics of leaders with charismatic effects: an extremely high level of self-confidence, dominance, and firm conviction in their beliefs (House 1976). However, what is intriguing is House's (1976) argument that while charismatic leaders present themselves highly confident with moral righteousness, it is possible that they do not indeed believe in either themselves or their beliefs. To mitigate this, "some leaders may thus have charismatic effects because of their ability to act as though they have such confidence and convictions" (p. 10). Still, according to Weber (1947), charismatic leaders are accepted by followers because they perceive the leader as possessing extraordinary powers.

One thing that most researchers agree on is that charismatic leadership has an emotional component to it, which then inspires followers to give the leader devotion, loyalty, and commitment (Antonakis 2012; Bass 1985; Bass and Riggio 2006; House 1976; Tucker 1968; Weber 1947). According to Weber (1947), the followers' relationship with the charismatic leader resembles a disciple to the master, where the leader is revered and admired. Tucker (1968) added to this argument by claiming that followers do not follow leaders "out of fear or monetary inducement, but out of love, passionate devotion, enthusiasm" (p. 735). Furthermore, what is typical of the followers' response to a charismatic leader is "not absolute obedience toward the leader, but simply the fact that by virtue of extraordinary qualities, he exercises a kind of 'domination' (as Weber puts it) over the followers" (p. 736).

Weber's (1947) theory of charismatic leadership is not without critique. Friedrich (1961) argued that Weber's (1947) notion of authority identified with legitimacy, specifically from followers' conformity, confused different situational factors. Some of the followers' conformity legitimizing the leader's authority could stem from the leader's personality traits, such as self-confidence, dominance, and self-rightness, and others from a simple positional power, such as the "head of Christendom or the Grand Llama" (Friedrich 1961, 13). He stressed that although several of these factors may be present concurrently, it is not permissible to confuse them. One of the biggest criticisms is around Weber's (1947) remark that charisma is a "crude swindle"—meaning, it can be used for good or bad, and regardless of the ethical considerations, what is most important when understanding this leadership concept is how it is valued by those who are ruled charismatically. Friedrich (1961) warned readers by saying, "We have here a striking instance of where the concern with being 'value-free' can lead eventually" (p. 15). He pointed out the dichotomy of the leadership impact of Hitler and Jesus Christ, Mussolini, and Moses, arguably all charismatic leaders, and emphasized that lumping them together is vastly misleading (Friedrich 1961). Therefore, researchers (Friedrich 1961; House 1976; Tucker 1968) suggested that future exploration should focus on the impact on others when evaluating the effectiveness of leader–follower relationships.

Consistent with transformational and charismatic leadership theories, leadership behaviors transform followers from self-focused to mission-focused (Antonakis 2012; Bass 1985; Bass and Riggio 2006; House 1976; Shamir et al. 1993; Tucker 1968; Weber 1947). However, Shamir et al. (1993) argued, "There is no motivational explanation to account for the profound effects of such leaders, some of which are difficult to explain within currently dominant models of motivation" (p. 578). They contend that charismatic leadership theory does not delineate how leadership enables profound effects on followers (Shamir et al. 1993). Therefore, examining self-concepts, specifically a closer look at how charismatic leaders activate self-concepts related to followers' motivations, is a critical component of relational leadership theory (Shamir et al. 1993).

Relational and Collective Self

Substantial research has been added to the entity perspective of the relational leadership theory by exploring the self-concept (Andersen and Chen 2002; Brewer and Gardner 1996; Hogg 2001; Knippenberg et al. 2005; Uhl-Bien 2006). It consists of two fundamental self-representations: the individual self and the collective self. The individual self includes those components of the self-concept that differentiate the self from all others (Brewer and Gardner 1996). These components include unique traits and characteristics that distinguish an individual in a social context. On the other hand, the work on the concept of the collective or social self, which Brewer and Gardner (1996) defined as "those aspects of the self-concept that reflect assimilation to others or significant social groups" (p. 83), highlights two distinct themes: relational and collective self.

Relational self stems from interpersonal relationships and interdependencies with significant others (Andersen and Chen 2002). These relationships include interpersonal bonds such as parent–child relationships, friendship or romantic relationships, and specific role relationships within the leader–follower context. On the other hand, the collective self is based on identity with a collective group (Uhl-Bien 2006). This form of self does not require personal relationships with others. It is derived from the relationship and interdependence with group membership in larger (Brewer and Gardner 1996). This self-concept is accentuated by differentiating the in-group one belongs to the out-groups, further emphasizing the sense of belonging (Hogg 2001). Integrating the individual self-concept with the two social extensions of the self, relational and collective, brings additional focus to various theories that shed light on how individuals define themselves in terms of their relationships with others and social groups (Brewer and Gardner 1996).

The Relational Self—An Interpersonal Social-Cognitive Theory

Andersen and Chen (2002) built their interpersonal social-cognitive theory on the existing work by Andersen and Glassman (1996), which explored how past experiences with significant individuals affect relationships with new people. Andersen and Chen (2002) claimed that the self is fundamentally relational and interdependent with the experiences people develop with significant others. They defined significant others as "any individual who is or has been deeply influential in one's life and in whom one is or once was emotionally invested" (Andersen and Chen 2002, 619).

Relationships with others shape the self-concept, whether these individuals are present physically or symbolically (Baldwin et al. 1990). Baldwin et al. (1990) suggested that self-evaluation involves a reflected appraisal process, where an individual assesses the self based on how significant others would likely think of them. Baldwin and Holmes (1987) conducted a study on undergraduate women subjects by asking some of them to visualize their parents' faces and others to visualize their friends' faces on campus. Then, under the guise of a separate study, the subjects were asked to rate the enjoyableness of a written passage that presented a permissive attitude toward sexuality. The study showed that women primed to first experience themselves with their parents rated the story significantly less enjoyable than those who visualized their friends from campus (Baldwin and Holmes 1987). This experiment demonstrated that individuals' memories with significant others could affect their sense of self, ultimately impacting their thoughts and behaviors (Baldwin and Holmes 1987).

Andersen and Chen (2002) stipulated, "self-knowledge is extensive and well-organized in memory" (p. 623), but given the extensive amount of knowledge one has about the self, one's entire body of self-knowledge cannot be cognitively accessible at once. Therefore, individuals can only access a subset of the total memory at any given moment, which Andersen and Chen (2002) called a working self-concept. They argued that this working self-concept guides individual cognition and behavior. Furthermore, because it is assumed that individuals have multiple significant others, there may also be a great deal of variability in how individuals visualize and experience self-concept with different significant others (Andersen and Chen 2002). Last, the self-concept is constructed based on a specific context. For example, a work environment may elicit one's "professional self," whereas a party setting may prompt the "partying self" concept (p. 623).

The central theme of Andersen's and Chen's (2002) interpersonal social-cognitive theory is that the "self is relational" (p. 619), intertwined with significant others. An individual's comprehensive collection of relational selves, stemming from all relationships, is a substantial source of interpersonal exchanges in everyday life.

The Collective Self—The Social Identity Theory of Leadership

Tajfel (1972) introduced the concept of social identity by theorizing how people see themselves within a group context. He pointed out three components of this process: categorization, identification, and comparison. Categorization refers to how individuals establish themselves by visually observing people and groups around them. Identification is the way individuals self-establish their unique identities. Last, comparison refers to the validation process to make one's identity obvious to in-group members and others (Tajfel 1972).

Hogg's (2001) work in the social identity theory of leadership focuses on the collective self to examine leadership as a group process.

According to Hogg (2001), while most researchers agree that "leadership is a relational property within groups" (p. 185), there is a scant academic analysis done on how leadership emerges through social cognitive processes associated with belonging to a group. Supporting this argument, an experiment conducted by Smith and Henry (1996) demonstrated that when a particular social identity is salient, individuals in a group are more likely to believe they possess the same characteristics of that social group. Hogg (2001) believed that leadership is a "structural feature of in-groups" (Hogg 2001, 186) and that "leaders and followers are interdependent roles embedded within a social system bounded by common group or category membership" (p. 186). His work on the group membership-oriented analysis of leadership promotes the idea that leaders can emerge from in-groups, maintain their positions, and affect followers and organizations as a result of social cognitive processes that cause people (a) to form their self-perceptions in terms of the defining attributes of an in-group; (b) to assimilate cognitively and behaviorally themselves to these in-group attributes (perceptions, attitudes, and feelings); and (c) to perceive others not as unique individuals but in comparison to the in-group stereotypes (Brewer and Gardner 1996; Hogg 2001; Uhl-Bien 2006).

Hogg (2001) introduced prototypicality, which refers to how leaders are perceived to match or embody the group characteristics. He argued that people categorize social contexts in terms of prototypes, readily accessible in individuals' memories. Hogg (2001) proposed that three factors operate concurrently "to make prototypicality an increasing influential basis of leadership processes as a function of increasing social identity salience" (p. 188).

The first factor is prototypicality. Hogg (2001) contended that as group members identify more strongly with the in-group, "prototypicality becomes an increasingly influential basis for leadership perceptions" (p. 189). These perceptions affect how leader–followers interact and form relationships (Andersen and Chen 2002; Brewer and Gardner 1996). Hogg (2001) claimed that people are susceptible to prototypicality within in-groups because it is the basis of perception and evaluation of self and other group members.

The second factor is social attraction within in-group dynamics, which refers to the phenomenon that people are more likely to agree or comply with someone if they like the individual (Berscheid and Reis 1998). Hogg (2001) stated, "Leadership is more than passively being a prototypical group member" (p. 189) and argued that leaders occupying prototypical positions, who are also socially attractive, are "able to exercise leadership by having his or her ideas accepted more readily and more widely than ideas suggested by others" (p. 189).

The third factor is attribution and information processing, which works with prototypicality and social attraction and helps individuals understand others' behaviors. According to Hogg (2001), "When group membership is salient, people are sensitive to prototypicality" (p. 190), and those group members who are most highly prototypical are considered more important. Therefore, these individuals attract more attention from others within a group context and are considered subjectively important. Hogg (2001) argued that in stable groups, over time, the behavior of a highly prototypical member is often attributed to the individual's personality traits rather than prototypicality. This tendency eventually results in viewing these individuals as charismatic, further distinguishing them from the rest of the group and giving them legitimacy as a leader (Hogg 2001).

Hogg's (2001) social identity of leadership theory fits well with the entity perspective of the relational leadership construct because exchanges among the group members occur in the collective dynamic that shapes the perceptions and behaviors of leaders and followers (Uhl-Bien 2006). Accompanying the relational conceptions of leadership theory is a growing interest in utilizing social network approaches to understand better how leaders' and followers' perceptions and behaviors are formed and ultimately shaped by relational exchanges (Balkundi and Kilduff 2005; Carter et al. 2015; Uhl-Bien 2006).

Social Networks

To integrate social network theory and leadership, Balkundi and Kilduff (2005) described social networks' vital role in influencing leaders within organizations. They proposed that followers' perceptions and behaviors are often manipulated by informal leaders within social networks, who can exercise social influence on group members. Leaders who do not understand the social structure and fail to anticipate its consequences leave their organizations vulnerable to the influences of these "skilled political entrepreneurs" (Balkundi and Kilduff 2005, 942).

> To be an effective leader of a social unit is to be aware of (a) the relations between actors in the unit; (b) the extent to which such relationships involve embedded ties, including kinship and friendship; (c) the extent to which social entrepreneurs are extracting value from their networks to facilitate or frustrate organizational goals; and (d) the extent to which the social structure of the unit includes cleavages between different factions. (Balkundi and Kilduff 2005, 946)

To illustrate this argument, Balkundi and Kilduff (2005) described a manufacturing company that experienced vandalism and many other disruptive acts, threatening the organization's future. Eventually, the management team discovered that these disruptive acts were conducted by the followers of a lower-ranked manager in the organization, who systemically recruited friends and family members for 30 years. The followers felt loyalty to this informal leader, thus creating a social network within the organization that was actively sabotaging the leadership team. This story demonstrates how "informal leaders who may lack formal authority can emerge to frustrate organizational functioning through the manipulation of network structures and the exercise of a social influence" (Balkundi and Kilduff 2005, 941).

Social network theory merges individual cognitive systems and complex structures of relationships consistent with the LMX and LMX-MMX theories (Balkundi and Kilduff 2005; Carter et al. 2015; Lord and Emrich 2001; Uhl-Bien 2006). The cognitive approach in individuals' minds draws attention to the central importance of cognitive structures—schema, a mental framework that helps individuals organize and interpret information and shape leadership perceptions and behaviors (Balkundi and Kilduff 2005). Lord and Emrich

(2001) emphasized the difference between individual and collective schemas, offering that collective cognition "reflects a socially constructed understanding of the world derived from social exchanges and interactions among multiple individuals in the group or organization" (Lord and Emrich 2001, 552). Cognitive systems theories, such as LMX and LMX-MMX, emphasize the importance of relations, particularly social structures and exchanges between leaders and followers (Balkundi and Kilduff 2005). By linking together social cognitions and social structures, Balkundi and Kilduff (2005) claimed to "forge a distinctive network approach to leadership that builds upon previous work in both the network and leadership realms" (p. 942).

At a glance, the social network approach fits more within the relational perspective because it considers relationships in the larger social and organizational contexts. However, it is still a part of the entity perspective because it approaches leadership from the individual perspective, their thoughts, feelings, and actions.

Leadership Impact on Organizations

In today's highly competitive business environment, organizations need the right leadership to survive and thrive (Galoji and Jibrin 2016). Katz and Miller (2014) claimed that there is an urgency for leaders to be different, to connect and inspire people, to help them connect work to the organization's purpose, and "to create a sense of safety so that people can bring their best selves to work" (p. 40). Katz and Miller (2014) argued that there is a paradigm shift in today's organizations and contended that relationship-oriented leaders with high EI can create collaborative and inclusive work environments. By doing so, they differentiate their organizations from those that do not adapt to this new leadership paradigm and subsequently fail.

Carter et al. (2015) presented a similar case for leadership as a foundational topic of organizational success, claiming that leadership is fundamentally relational. However, they added that leadership enables organizations to function by "directing, inspiring, and coordinating the efforts of individuals, teams, and organizations toward the realization of collective goals" (Carter et al. 2015, 597). In other words, in addition to the perceived value of the relational approach, the emphasis is placed on leaders' effectiveness in achieving collective organizational goals. Effective leadership is often viewed as the foundation for organizational performance (Bass 1985; Galoji and Jibrin 2016; Katzenbach and Smith 1999). Hence, "Organizations that fail to have effective leadership may likely fail to meet performance expectations" (Galoji and Jibrin 2016, 157).

Although the two perspectives mentioned above are similar, they touch on two distinct themes: relational leaders affecting organizations through self-efficacy and EI. Both themes fit well within the entity perspective of the relational leadership theory as they deal with a leader's cognitive and emotional abilities as an individual entity. The following section explores these two topics.

Self-Efficacy

There is substantial evidence through the works of various researchers for the strong connection between self-efficacy and human performance (Anderson et al. 2008; Galoji and Jibrin 2016; Judge et al. 2007; Semadar et al. 2006; Stajkovic and Luthans 1998). Bandura (1977, 1978) claimed that individuals acquire, regulate, and retain new behavior patterns through cognitive processes. He defined these cognitive processes as "thinking processes involved in the acquisition, organization, and use of information" (Bandura 1977, 71). Contending that these cognitive processes influence human learning and motivation, he offered the theory of self-efficacy, an individual's belief in self-capacity to execute behaviors necessary to produce specific performance attainments (Bandura 1977, 1978).

In elaborating on the relationship between self-efficacy and performance, Bandura (1977) distinguished a concept of efficacy expectation, which he defined as "a person's estimate that a given behavior will lead to certain outcomes" (p. 193). In this context, the outcome is differentiated from efficacy expectation. While individuals may believe that a particular course of action may lead to a specific outcome, such information does not influence their behavior if they doubt their abilities to perform the necessary activities to reach their ultimate goal (Bandura 1977). This concept can be illustrated by describing a common understanding of exercise and diet leading to weight loss. While it is widely accepted that exercise and diet lead to weight loss, such information may be disregarded by individuals who believe they may be unable to cope with dieting or exercising. Bandura (1977) stated that people engage in situations they think they can handle and avoid others that intimidate them. Therefore, self-belief, or in this context, efficacy expectation, is a crucial determinant of performance.

Bandura and Jourden (1991) argued that self-belief of efficacy is a fundamental driver in individuals' decision making. Individuals with a strong self-belief of efficacy set higher goals for themselves while exhibiting a higher level of commitment toward attaining those goals (Bandura and Jourden 1991; Latham and Locke 1991; Locke and Latham 1990; Wood and Bandura 1989).

Bandura (1977) elaborated on the relationship between efficacy expectancy and performance, stating, "In most studies, the measures of expectations are mainly concerned with people's hopes for favorable outcomes rather than with their sense of personal mastery" (p. 194). He argued that efficacy expectations differ in several ways. Magnitude is one dimension of variability, which refers to the degree of difficulty an individual feels is required to perform a particular task. While some experiences create specific mastery expectations, others instill a more generalized sense of efficacy beyond a particular situation. Bandura (1977) referred to this dimension as a generality. Finally, expectancies vary in strength. Individuals who possess a strong expectation of mastery will persevere through negative experiences. Bandura (1977) suggested that both performance and efficacy expectations should be observed closely to assess their reciprocal effects because "mastery expectations influence performance and are, in turn, altered by cumulative effects of one's efforts" (p. 194).

Shavelson and Bolus (1982) claimed that self-perceptions of competence are integral to self-concepts. Consistent with this view, Bandura (1977, n.d.) offered four primary sources of influence for people's beliefs about their efficacy. According to Bandura (1977, n.d.), the most effective way to create strong self-efficacy is through experiencing success. The old maxim of success breeds more success fits well within this concept. Furthermore, Bandura (1977) proposed that after individuals build strong self-efficacy through repeated success, the impact on self-efficacy from a negative experience or an occasional failure is significantly low. Bandura (1977) also warned that repeated failures could lower self-efficacy. The effect of early and repeated success and failure on self-efficacy and collective efficacy (Pajares 1997) is especially noteworthy within the leadership context because the accountability shifts on leaders' ability to create environments where their followers engage in positive experiences (Antonakis 2012; Bass 1985, 1999; Burns 1978; Katz and Miller 2014).

The second way to create strong self-belief is through "the vicarious experiences provided by social models" (Bandura n.d., 2). Seeing others perform a task successfully builds certain self-expectations in individuals. Bandura (1977) further claimed, "Seeing others perform threatening activities without adverse consequences can generate expectations in observers that they too will improve if they intensify and persist in their efforts" (p. 197). A fitting illustration of this concept is Roger Bannister's 1954 record of running a mile in less than 4 minutes. Before Bannister broke this record, running a mile in less than 4 minutes was considered impossible (Bannister 2014). While Bannister's new world record was a significant historical event in middle-distance running, what is equally noteworthy is that within 2 months after Bannister's record, two more athletes ran a mile in less than 4 minutes. In the 67 years after Bannister broke the 4-minute barrier, 1400 athletes ran 1 mile in less than 4 minutes, and Bannister's record was lowered by almost 17 seconds.

According to Bandura (1977), the remaining two factors that build self-efficacy are social persuasion and emotional arousal. Self-efficacy through social persuasion occurs when individuals are verbally persuaded that they possess the capabilities to master a particular task. Authentic suggestions that enable the recipients to believe "they can cope successfully with what has overwhelmed them in the past" (Bandura 1977, 198) positively impact self-efficacy. According to

Bandura (1977), authentic suggestions are rooted in emotional arousal. While eliciting fear can create a stressful situation and debilitate one's self-belief, positive and authentic encouragement can lead individuals to higher self-efficacy (Lick and Bootzin 1975; Moore 1965; Paul 1966). Bandura (1977) claimed that in stressful situations, especially with negative feedback, individuals with low self-efficacy exude a significantly lower effort toward a task that is perceived to be difficult. Alternatively, individuals with high self-efficacy will persist in mastering the challenge during stressful situations, even if their feedback is negative. Based on the above evidence, EI is crucial in leaders' understanding of their emotions and motivations and those around them. A leader with a high EI will diagnose and manage personal emotions and recognize and moderate emotional disturbances in others, which ultimately positively affects individual and organizational performance (Seipp 1991). The following section closely examines the role of EI in the relational context.

Emotional Intelligence

In exploring the role emotions play in people's daily lives, Bradberry and Greaves (2009) found that only 36 percent of the 500,000 surveyed could accurately identify their emotions as they were experiencing them. Reflecting on these findings, Bradberry and Greaves (2009) stated, "Two-thirds of us are typically controlled by our emotions and are not yet skilled at spotting them and using them to our benefit" (p. 13). The implications of this survey are staggering, especially in the context of relational leadership.

While the contemporary theory of EI was first introduced by Salovey and Mayer (1990) and later popularized by Goleman (1995), the concept of EI has been evolving for more than a century. To find a widely accepted practical definition for human intelligence, Thorndike (1920) offered three distinct concepts: (a) mechanical intelligence, which he defined as the ability to learn about and manage everyday things and mechanisms, such as a knife and a fork, or an automobile and a lawn mower; (b) abstract intelligence, which refers to a human being's ability to comprehend, communicate, and utilize ideas and symbols, such as words and numbers; and (c) social intelligence, which he referred to as the "ability to understand and manage men and women, boys and girls—to act wisely in human relations" (Thorndike 1920, 228).

Building on Thorndike's (1920) work, researchers offered various constructs on human intelligence (Chapin 1942; Doll 1935; Moss and Hunt 1927; Wechsler 1943, 1958). Eventually, the attention shifted from assessing social intelligence to understanding interpersonal behavior and its role in human effectiveness (Bar-On 2006; Goleman 1995; Salovey and Mayer 1990). Moss and Hunt (1927) argued, "People neither born equal, live equal, nor die equal" (p. 108), claiming the main differentiator is the ability to get along with others. Wechsler (1958) referred to this type of intelligence as "the capacity of the individual to act purposefully" (p. 7).

In their seminal work, Salovey and Mayer (1990) described EI as the individual's ability to perceive, manage, understand, and facilitate using emotions. Salovey and Mayer (1990) viewed EI and social intelligence as parts of the same construct. However, Goleman (1998) saw social intelligence as a "threshold capability" (p. 2), claiming that IQ and technical skills are more like "the entry-level requirements for executive positions" (p. 2). Goleman (1998) argued that most effective leaders have one thing in common, "they have a high degree of what has come to be known as emotional intelligence" (p. 1). Goleman (1998) claimed that EI not only distinguishes superior leaders but also leads to solid performance. In the article "What Makes a Leader," Goleman (1998) pointed out the results of McClelland's (1966, as cited in Goleman 1998) study of a global food and beverage company, which demonstrated that "when senior managers had a critical mass of emotional intelligence capabilities, their divisions outperformed yearly earnings goals by 20 percent" (Goleman 1998, 2).

According to Goleman and Boyatzis (2017), EI has four dimensions: self-awareness, self-management, social awareness, and relationship management. Though different researchers refer to them by other names (Gardner 1983; Goleman 1995; Mayer and Salovey 1997), the four dimensions are shared by most EI theories. In providing further clarity on the construct. Goleman (1998) offered five components of EI, which he refer to as "learned and learnable capabilities that allow outstanding performance at work or as a leader" (Goleman and Boyatzis 2017, 3).

Goleman (1998) claimed that one of the most critical components of EI is self-awareness, which means "having a deep understanding of one's emotions, strengths, weaknesses, needs, and drives" (p. 3). Individuals with high self-awareness not only identify their own emotions in each moment, but also recognize how their emotions affect others. Highly self-aware individuals are conscious of emotional triggers that elicit negative or positive reactions. They can speak about their emotions "accurately and openly—although not necessarily effusively or confessionally" (Goleman 1998, 5). Because self-reflection is a critical component of self-awareness (Bolman and Deal 2017), leaders must continuously challenge the beliefs that limit them to familiar ways of thinking (Senge 1990). Self-reflection helps leaders increase self-understanding, reduce self-consciousness, and increase awareness of one's priorities (Lanaj et al. 2019).

The second component of EI is self-regulation (Goleman 1995, 1998). Recognizing one's emotions is insufficient to be an effective leader; self-regulation to manage one's emotions is equally critical (Goleman 1995). Goleman (1998) claimed that individuals who can self-regulate feelings can build an environment of trust and fairness. He argued that organizations with such cultures can attract and retain top talent. Furthermore, Goleman (1998) claimed that in today's ever-changing business environment, where ambiguity is a norm, organizations that have leaders who have high self-regulation can "roll with the changes" (p. 6) and bring their employees along. Goleman (1995, 1998) contended that the signs of high emotional self-regulation are as follows: "a propensity for reflection and thoughtfulness; comfort with ambiguity and change; and integrity—an ability to say no to impulsive urges" (Goleman 1998, 6).

Goleman (1998) claimed that motivation is another component of high EI. He proposed that motivation is one trait of all leaders and that "they display an unflagging energy to do things better" (p. 7). Individuals with high motivation remain positive in the face of adversity. Additionally, they can transfer this disposition to their peers and followers, positively affecting organizational performance.

The third component of EI is empathy, which Goleman (1998) claimed to be the most recognizable dimension. Empathetic leaders carefully consider their employees' feelings and other factors and make sound decisions. In the era of globalization, cross-cultural interactions sometimes lead to miscommunications, which can destabilize a team and the organization. Goleman (1998) contended that "empathy is an antidote" (p. 8) to such issues. Highly empathetic leaders can read the nonverbal cues and connect with individuals more deeply.

According to Goleman (1995, 1998), social skills are EI's last and arguably most complex components. Along with empathy, social skills help individuals manage relationships with others (Goleman 1998). According to Goleman (1998), social skills differ from being simply friendly. He claimed:

> Socially skilled people tend to have a wide circle of acquaintances, and they have a knack for finding common ground with people of all kinds—a knack for building rapport. That does not mean they socialize continually; it means they work according to their assumption that nothing important gets done alone. Such people have a network in place when the time of action comes (Goleman 1998, 9).

EI is consistent with the entity perspective of relational leadership. It focuses on individuals as stand-alone entities and their abilities to understand and manage personal and other's feelings. The relational component is rooted in Goleman's (1995, 1998, 2004) works because leaders with high EI can forge relationships with others to make better decisions and solve complex problems (Yukl 2010). Such leaders are highly counted on in organizations because they are "exquisitely sensitive to the impact they are having on others and seamlessly adjust their styles to get the best results" (Goleman 2004, 87).

In summary, the entity perspective views relational leadership from the standpoint of individual perceptions, behaviors, and exchanges. It focuses on the traits and characteristics of leaders and followers and views leadership from the lenses of manager–subordinate and leader–follower exchanges that influence one another. The emerging work in relational leadership theory builds on the entity perspective and approaches leadership from the standpoint of a process engaged by many participants in a nonstatic, evolving social and organizational context (Uhl-Bien 2006). The next chapter highlights this approach, framing it from the relational perspective.

CHAPTER 6

The Relational Perspective

Traditional relational leadership research is rooted in exploring what leaders do or ought to do to create relational environments and what leadership characteristics or styles help create relational processes (e.g., Bass 1999; Bass and Riggio 2006; Block 2006; Burns 1978; Drath 1990; House 1976). While leadership process concepts extended to dyads or leader–follower exchanges, such as LMX theory (Graen and Uhl-Bien 1995), individual leader-centric contracts are central to entitative perspective theories.

In contrast to the theories composing the entity perspective, the relational perspective promotes that attention should be switched from leaders, as individuals, and from their actions to leadership, as a dynamic social process created by equally valued and empowered players (Dachler and Hosking 1995a; Hosking 1988; Uhl-Bien 2006). The key focus of this approach is to seek the understanding of the process of leadership creation, which Uhl Bien (2006) defined as "the influential acts of organizing that contribute to the structuring of interactions and relationships" (p. 662). The following sections explore this social process and delineate theories that fit the relational perspective model.

Relational Constructionism—Multiple Reality

The most prominent work on relational perspectives of the RLT is that of Hosking, Dachler, and colleagues (Brown and Hosking 1986; Dachler and Hosking 1995a; Hosking 1988; Hosking and Pluut 2010). Dachler and Hosking (1995a) claimed that to better understand the underlying epistemology of the relational perspective, it is best to contrast it with the epistemological assumptions of the entity approach. They suggested that entity perspective, which they call possessive individualism, has two epistemological themes. The first assumption is that the "knowing individual, in principle, is understood as an entity" (Dachler and Hosking 1995a, 2). Consistent with Cartesian philosophy, under this assumption, an individual is endowed with a knowing mind, and knowledge is viewed as the individual's property. Following this logic, individuals are understood to possess properties such as personality traits, characteristics, and expert knowledge (Dachler and Hosking 1995a). The second assumption stems from the first one. Specifically, individual possessions, including interests and goals, act as the control mechanisms of internal and external nature, which includes other people (Dachler and Hosking 1995b; Gergen 1994; von Glasersfeld 1985). To summarize, according to the possessive individualism construct, knowing entities utilize their possessions to influence and control the internal and external nature around them (Dachler and Hosking 1995a). Consistent with these assumptions, Dachler and Hosking (1995a) proposed that social relations are viewed as subject–object relationships since people are integral to external nature.

Dachler and Hosking (1995a) claimed that entity perspective-oriented theories imply such context in which leaders are understood as subjects set apart from the objects, including followers, followers' tasks, and organizations. Furthermore, in this context of seeing relationships as subject–object exchanges, a leader's "goals and interests are privileged relative to those of the objects of leadership" (Dachler and Hosking 1995a, 8), and the leader is the "architect and controller of the internal and external order" (p. 2) within the array of individual possessions— his followers. By implication, subordinates, as objects of leadership, are less knowledgeable about the leader's privileged goals and interests; therefore, they cannot be as self-developed and self-responsible as the leader. Instead, leaders are the activators and organizers of the followers' motivations, compliance, and success (Dachler and Hosking 1995a).

While some entity perspective-oriented theories may appear less individualistic (e.g., LMX), the implicit assumptions highlighted above remain. However, within relational epistemology, leaders' traits and attributes and ability to influence followers do not matter. From the relational perspective, the question is how particular communally agreed-upon leadership enactments are created (Dachler and Hosking

1995a). Dachler and Hosking (1995a) offered that such communally enacted leadership concepts are different from when a leader, who thinks it motivates followers, asks for suggestions from subordinates, and then integrates some of the recommendations into action. These types of actions reflect the entitative perspective. Instead, the relational perspective promotes a partnership model for leadership where there is no inference of self as subject and others as objects. Dachler and Hosking (1995a) proposed, "The partnership model can only make sense by reference to the fundamental epistemological assumptions of the relational perspective" (p. 9).

Knowledge and Meaning-Making

Von Glasersfeld (1989) defined knowledge as a commodity fundamentally different from objective representation. He argued that human beings construct their subjective reality and claimed that for constructivists, knowledge is a "conceptual structure that epistemic agents, given the range of present experience within their tradition of thought and language, consider viable" (Von Glasersfeld 1989, 124). For Von Glasersfeld (1989), constructivism is a "form of pragmatism and shared with it the attitudes toward knowledge and truth" (p. 124).

Knowledge is one area that the relational perspective views as socially contracted and socially distributed instead of individual possession, consistent with the entitative perspective. Dachler and Hosking (1995a) suggested that in the philosophical tradition of hermeneutics and various studies on interpreting the meaning of literature, whose authors are no longer available for a conversation, the text refers to a written document from which knowledge is gleaned. However, they argued that these texts in themselves are equivocal, and they acquire meaning "only to the extent that they can be related, through narration and conversations, with ongoing stories in the social/cultural context" (p. 5). In contrast, with the entitative perspective, which views knowledge as an individual possession, Dachler and Hosking (1995a) proposed that knowledge and knowing "is always a process of relating and meaning making" (p. 5). Therefore, within the context of knowledge-making and knowledge-sharing, Dachler and Hosking (1995a) rejected the concept of one entity being in a superior position over others. The argument is that exchanging ideas and conversations about facts, texts, and events creates ongoing relational constructions.

Coordination of Action

In the entity perspective, coordination of action is a social process in which the leader's voice is one among many, and the responsibility for enacting relational processes is equally distributed among leaders and followers (Brown and Hosking 1986; Dachler and Hosking 1995a; Gronn 2009; Hosking and Pluut 2010). Gronn (2009) viewed the concept of equal responsibility as distributed leadership. He claimed that leadership should be viewed as a holistic entity, fluid and emergent rather than a fixed phenomenon. Calling such a process of leadership "concerted action" (p. 252), Gronn illustrated his argument with three different forms of engagement: (a) spontaneous collaboration, (b) intuitive working relationships, and (c) institutionalized practices. Spontaneous collaboration is when leadership practice arises in response to a particular issue or a set of circumstances, requiring participants with various skills and knowledge to work together (Gronn 2009). In this scenario, the collaboration may cease once the problem is solved. However, it can set in motion future collaboration opportunities (Gronn 2009; Thorpe et al. 2011). Intuitive working relationships are formed when at least two participants mutually rely on each other, where mutual trust is crucial. In this scenario, participants intuitively discover the benefits of distributive leadership and followership (Thorpe et al. 2011). Last, institutionalized practice occurs when learning from spontaneous collaboration and intuitive working practices are formalized as organizational knowledge (Gronn 2009). The concept of institutionalized practice is also thoroughly documented in the works of Kotter (1990, 1995, 1996), who viewed institutionalization as the last step in his uroboros 8-step organizational change model.

Dachler and Hosking's (1995a) model of coordination of action, while analogous to Gronn's (2009) concerted action construct, acts as a prerequisite for the relational leadership process. According to Dachler and Hosking (1995a):

The relational epistemology, by recognizing knowledge as socially distributed and truth as socially certified, does not privilege any particular knowledge claim as more true.... Multiple realities, in the sense of multiple meanings, descriptions of knowledge claims are a part of the local ontology in the process of being narrated.... Reality is no longer viewed as a singular fact of nature but as multiple and socially constructed (p. 6).

According to Dachler and Hosking (1995a), for coordination of action, all parties need to agree that knowledge can only be discovered collectively and that no individual can be the sovereign author of it. Dachler and Hosking (1995a) suggested that knowledge is a process of relating and can only be discovered through multiloguing—a term they coined to describe the process of speaking of many concerning many contexts in the relational perspective. Drath (2001) aligned with the concept of multiloguing by proposing that leadership is a relational dialogue—a process in which leaders and followers exchange ideas to construct what Senge (1990) called learning organizations.

Sociocultural Limits

A key concept in relational epistemology is that multiloguing dramatically broadens meaning-making possibilities (Dachler and Hosking 1995a). However, certain sociocultural elements may ignore and restrict particular perspectives and label them undesirable or wrong if they do not fit the accepted narrative. Relational epistemology ignores these sociocultural contexts by focusing on knowledge being discovered only through many voices participating in a social process (Dachler and Hosking 1995a). An example of this conflict is historically subdued feminine voices in social, organizational, and world affairs in the context of masculine cultures. Gilligan (1982) pointed out that the problem with understanding women's points of view stems from the differences observed in how men and women experience relationships. Gilligan (1982) started her theory by pointing out Freud's (1914, as cited in Gilligan, 1982) essay "On Narcissism," where he discussed the concept of capacity to love by contrasting love for the mother and love for the self, calling this dichotomy "dividing the world of love into narcissism and object relationships" (p. 24). According to Gilligan (1982), Freud found that "while men's development becomes clearer, women's becomes increasingly opaque" (as cited in Gilligan 1982, 24). The problem, Gilligan (1982) claimed, arises because contrasting love between mother and self yields two different images of relationships. She stated, "Relying on the imagery of men's lives in charting the course of human growth, Freud is unable to trace in women the development of relationships, morality, or a clear sense of self" (p. 24). Freud's deep-rooted prejudices about women and his infamous comment about the dark continent of psychology regarding women's sexuality are consistent with the issue highlighted by Dachler and Hosking (1995a) that certain perspectives may be ignored because of the inability to understand within a certain sociocultural context.

In summary, there are multiple realities at work in the entitative and relational approaches of the relational leadership theory, each having a legitimate place in creating a relational environment. While both perspectives emphasize relationships, how they view and pursue building relationships differ significantly. While the entity perspective draws from the individual viewpoint, with the leader as a focal point, the relational perspective views leadership as a shared social process, where leaders' and followers' effects on each other are equally valued. In this construct, knowledge is not centered as more or less subjective or objective in one individual's mind (Hosking and Pluut 2010). The ontology is given to relational processes and the local realities they create. The term "local" is employed here as a process through which relational realities are made and remade (Hosking and Pluut 2010). What is real in this postentity perspective is emergent relational interactions that continuously change and evolve. To borrower Chia's (1995) words, relational constructionism assumes an "ontology of becoming" rather than the "ontology of being" (p. 581).

CHAPTER 7

Central Themes of Relational Leaders

Upon comprehensive examination of scholarly literature on relational leadership, which has been exhaustively discussed in the preceding chapters, several recurring traits inherent to relational leaders have repeatedly surfaced. Following synthesizing these prevalent themes, four overarching principles have emerged, delineating relational leaders as culture creators, influencers, inclusive, and engaging. It is imperative to clearly define each of these characteristics based on the insights gleaned from various theorists on relational leadership.

- *Culture creators:* Individuals who lead with values and inspire others around them, leaders and followers alike, to help each other advance to a higher level of motivation.
- *Influencer:* People who possess high levels of social and relational connectivity with others and strong professional and charismatic capabilities.
- *Inclusive:* Leaders who actively embrace the deliberate and continual practice of welcoming individuals from diverse backgrounds to participate in every aspect of organizational work, including holding leadership positions and contributing to decision-making processes.
- *Engaging:* Leaders who inspire followers to get involved in the organization's success and be enthusiastic and committed to their work and workplace.

Figure 7.1 provides a comprehensive overview detailing the authors whose writings substantiate these characteristics, offering invaluable insights into the multifaceted dimensions of relational leadership. Leader practitioners keen on broadening their understanding of various

Culture Creators	Influencers	Inclusive	Engaging
Antonakis (2012)	Andersen and Chen (2002)	Antonakis (2012)	Andersen and Chen (2002)
Bandura (1977, 1994)	Anderson et al. (2008)	Balkundi and Kil duff	Andersen and Glassman
Bar-On (2006)	Antonakis (2012)	(2005)	(1996)
Bass (1985, 1999)	Bandura (1994)	Bandura (1978)	Avolio et al. (2009)
Bass and Riggio (2006)	Bandura and Jourden	Bar-On (2006)	Baldwin et al. (1990)
Bass and Steidlmeier	(1991)	Bass (1999)	Baldwin and Holmes
(1999)	Bannister (2014)	Bass and Steidlmeier	(1987)
Beverly (2016)	Bass (1985, 1995a, 1999)	(1999)	Balkundi and Kilduff
Block (2006)	Bass and Riggio (2006)	Beverly (2016)	(2005)
Bolman and Deal (2017)	Berscheid and Reis (1998)	Block (2006)	Bass (1985)
Bryman (1993)	Bryman (1993)	Brower et al. (2000)	Beverly (2016)
Burns (1978)	Burns (1978)	Brown and Hosking (1986)	Brewer and Gardner (1996)
Carter et al. (2015)	Coetzer et al. (2017)	Chia (1995)	Brower et al. (2000)
Dachler and Hosking	Fiol et al. (1999)	Coetzer et al. (2017)	Burns (1978)
(1995a)	French and Raven (1959)	Dachler and Hosking	Carter et al. (2015)
Dansereau et al. (1975)	Galoji and Jibrin (2016)	(1995 a)	Chia (1995)
Dewar et al. (2020)	Goleman (1995)	Dansereau et al. (1975)	Dachler and Hosking
Drath (1990)	Hogg (2001)	Dewar et al. (2020)	(1995a)
Fiol et al. (1999)	House (1976)	Fiol et al. (1999)	Dansereau et al. (1975)
Gajendran and Aparna	Judge et al. (2007)	Gajendran and Aparna	Dewar et al. (2020)
(2012)	Katz and Miller (2014)	(2012)	Drath (1990)
Greenleaf (1977)	Katzenbach and Smith	Goleman (1995)	Fiol et al. (1999)
Hollander (1992, 2010)	(1999)	Graen (2016)	Friedrich (1961)
House (1976)	Lanaj et al. (2019)	Greenleaf (1977)	Gajendran and Aparna
Katz and Miller (2014)	Latham and Locke (1991)	Hogg (2001)	(2012)
Kirkpatrick and Locke	Lewin (1947)	Katz and Miller (2014)	Galoji and Jibrin (2016)
(1991)	Lord and Emrich (2001)	Lick and Bootzin (1975)	Goleman (1995, 1998)
Kotter (1995)	Lunenburg (2010)	McCall et al. (1988)	Graen (2016)
Lewin (1947)	McCall et al. (1988)	Moore (1965)	Graen and Uhl-Bien (1995)
Murrell (1997)	Moss and Hunt (1927)	Pajares (1997)	Graham (1991)
Patterson (2003)	Roberto (2005)	Paul (1966)	Greenleaf (1977)
Power (2013)	Rockstuhl (2012)	Power (2013)	Hogg (2001)
Roberto (2005)	Seipp (1991)	Roberto (2005)	Hollander (1992, 2010)
Rockstuhl (2012)	Senge (1990)	Rockstuhl (2012)	Hosking (1988)
Russell and Stone (2002)	Shamir et al. (1993)	Russell and Stone (2002)	Hosking and Pluut (2010)
Salovey and Mayer (1990)	Stajkovic and Luthans	Senge (1990)	Katz and Miller (2014)
Schyns and Day (2010)	(1998)	Shamir et al. (1993)	Knippenberg et al. (2005)
Senge (1990)	Tucker (1968)	Smith and Henry (1996)	Lord and Emrich (2001)
Shamir et al. (1993)	Weber (1947)	Tajfel (1972)	Mayer and Salovey (1997)
Spears (2010)	Yukl (1999)	Uhl-Bien (2006)	Patterson (2003)
Thorpe et al. (2011)		Van Dierendonck (2011)	Power (2013)
Tracey and Hinkin (1998)			Salovey and Mayer (1990)
Uhl-Bien (2006)			Thorndike (1920)
Van Dierendonck (2011)			Thorpe et al. (2011)
			Tracey and Hinkin (1998)

Figure 7.1 Central themes of relational leadership and authors

models within relational leadership theories can delve into these scholarly writings to further enrich their knowledge and expertise.

Drawing from the theorists listed in Figure 7.1, relational leaders embodying the four common characteristics of culture creators, influencers, inclusive, and engaging cultivate organizational cultures where leaders and followers are empowered to bring forth their best versions, contributing to creating a high-quality workplace environment.

While the comparative analysis between these theoretical findings and the subsequent research data points are detailed in Chapter 10, it was no surprise to see the central themes of relational leaders as culture creators and influencers. It is important to note that according to various leadership theorists, relational leaders fundamentally build cultures by influencing others. However, data suggest they achieve this influence not through corporate roles and titles or manipulative managerial tactics but through genuine personal connections and openness to inclusivity that magnetically draws people to them. Although it's premature to draw definitive conclusions at this stage, I couldn't help but draw a parallel between these theoretical findings and the leaders I encountered in my career, who positively impacted me and many others around me. These leaders created a culture of highly engaged stakeholders who freely received as much value from the leaders as they contributed to the organization. From a theoretical standpoint, this mutually beneficial dynamic fosters a trust-based workplace culture, leading to high stakeholder engagement at all levels of the organization, enabling leaders, followers, and their organizations to thrive together.

CHAPTER 8

Stop, Collaborate, and Listen

In Chapters 5 and 6, we exhaustively covered relational leadership theories from both entity and relational perspectives. These chapters provided a comprehensive understanding of relational leadership's foundational concepts and different approaches. In Chapter 7, we extracted and defined common characteristics of relational leaders from various theoretical writings. This analysis allowed us to identify critical traits consistently highlighted in the literature as common traits of relational leaders. With such a solid theoretical foundation, our next endeavor was to juxtapose these theoretical findings against real-life situations. This involved examining how practicing leaders exhibit relational leadership traits in real-life situations.

In pursuit of this objective, meticulously constructed qualitative research was orchestrated, characterized by a rigorous and systematic approach aimed at addressing a set of precisely delineated research questions. The ensuing data, amassed through a scrupulously detailed and methodologically sound process, underwent an exhaustive and multifaceted analysis. This analytical rigor was unwaveringly aligned with the established methodological framework, ensuring the sustained integrity, reliability of the study's empirical findings, and the credibility of the conclusions.

I don't blame you if you felt confused after reading the last paragraph and thought I was speaking in riddles. This confusion underscores a common disconnect between scholarly research and its practical application. In the first chapter, I mentioned that while the book is rooted in scholarly research, it aims to provide leaders with valuable tools to enhance their personal and organizational effectiveness amidst the VUCA business environment. However, to draw credible conclusions, we must rely on a well-designed research study that follows specific methodological rules. Unfortunately, such studies are often written in a way that's hard for nonresearch experts to understand, as they are predominantly meant for academia. Most practicing leaders, however, are not familiar with the complexities of scholarly research writing. Even if one delves deep into reading various research publications on leadership, it may still be puzzling why the language is so convoluted and ambiguous if the goal is to improve leadership practice. This is likely why many academic studies on leadership rarely make it into practical application.

In the subsequent section of this chapter, I aim to simplify the complex research design language to advance practical knowledge of relational leadership. Let's look at how the study was designed in a way that won't leave us pulling our hair out.

It was late October of 1990, and the music charts were dominated by pop artists such as Mariah Carey, Janet Jackson, and Madonna. But for seven days of glory, Vanilla Ice was number one with his first single hit song, "Ice Ice Baby." Despite its stolen beats, lackluster rapping, and peculiarly niche references, the song permeated the American culture. The iconic lyric—stop, collaborate, and listen, which has become a pop culture catchphrase over the years—may also serve as insight into how the song was created. Using samples of other artists' works, which were started and stopped throughout the song, could represent the word *stop* in the lyric. Additionally, while Vanilla Ice was initially credited as the sole writer of the lyrics for "Ice Ice Baby," it later came to light that the song contained similarities to the bassline of "Under Pressure" by Queen and David Bowie. As a result, credit for the "Ice Ice Baby" bassline was officially shared with the writers of "Under Pressure"—Queen's Freddie Mercury, Brian May, John Deacon, Roger Taylor, and David Bowie. Hence, the song references collaboration. The word *listen* is perhaps how we, the audience, interpret the song's various elements.

Ironically, designing a research study on relational leadership theory closely resembled crafting the lyrics of a song analogous to Ice Ice Baby, naturally, minus the act of appropriating sources and intellectual property. Similar to how Vanilla Ice incorporated samples of other artists' works into his song, our examination of scholarly writings in Chapters 5 and 6 serves as a pause to analyze and reflect on various scholarly writings on relational leadership. Moreover, to emphasize the collaborative nature of this endeavor, this chapter invites readers to evaluate the research design and review the steps taken to execute the study. This includes defining the research questions that guided our inquiry, explaining how we collected and analyzed data, and discussing the methods used to ensure the study's credibility and reliability of the findings. Finally, much like the emphasis on the word *listen* in "Ice Ice Baby," our goal as scholar-practitioners is to actively listen to real-life leaders' insights on applying the relational leadership model in practice. Subsequently, we compare these leadership practices with the central themes derived from the scholarly literature highlighted in Chapter 7 and bridge any gaps between these data points.

Purpose of the Study

The study aimed to understand what relational leadership strategies are currently employed among leaders focused on developing quality workplace environments. Additionally, the study investigated how relational leaders influence people around them to create inclusive and engaging cultures. By gaining a deeper understanding of relational leadership and its positive benefits in creating inclusive and engaging organizational cultures, leaders will be better equipped to lead their teams and navigate their organizations in this ever-changing, highly competitive VUCA business climate.

Research Questions

The main question for this study was:

- What relational leadership strategies are commonly practiced by leaders to foster quality workplace environments?

Subquestions

- Research Question 1: What relational leadership strategies are commonly practiced by leaders to create quality organizational cultures?
- Research Question 2: What relational leadership strategies are commonly practiced by leaders to influence others?
- Research Question 3: What relational leadership strategies are commonly practiced by leaders to create inclusivity?
- Research Question 4: What relational leadership strategies are commonly practiced by leaders to create employee and organizational engagement?

Methods

Uhl-Bien's (2006) relational leadership theory provided the theoretical framework for this research study. The study employed a qualitative design utilizing narratives in the data collection process. A choice for the qualitative approach was substantiated by the scant amount of research on how leaders employ relational leadership style to create quality workplace environments. Narratives gathered through publicly available and accessible sources such as books, magazines, newspaper articles, blogs, and recorded presentations, which offer glimpses into leaders' thoughts and behaviors, were collected and analyzed in relation to the study's purpose. The themes gleaned from the data were reviewed for alignment with the key characteristics of relational leaders uncovered during the extensive literature review: culture creators, influencers, inclusive, and engaging.

Ethical Considerations

Because "the research involves collecting data about people" (as cited in Creswell and Creswell 2018, 88), a central ethical consideration in this study was maintaining the anonymity of individuals. For this purpose, the researcher did not use the individuals' names and titles or anything else to recognize the organizations where they work. Instead, the researcher referred to individuals in the study simply as leaders.

To further protect anonymity, the researcher obfuscated the obtained data without materially changing the information and assigned a numeric number to each researched leader. For example, the first source utilized for the first research question was notated as A1, the second source as A2, the third as A3, and so on. Only the researcher held the list of obtained sources in an electronic folder, saved in the private, password-protected computer, shared with the research panel for review, and later destroyed upon completion of the study.

In relating the concept of justice toward subjects, researchers ensured that participants were selected equitably based on factors relevant to the study. To ensure that the selection process of subjects was equitable, the researcher drew candidates from a large pool of nationwide leaders from multiple publicly available and accessible sources, including published books, websites, journals, and news articles.

Data Sources and Data Gathering Procedures

Because the data for the study was gathered from publicly available and accessible texts, there was no interaction with human subjects, and, therefore, the study qualified as nonhuman subjects' research. The number of sources obtained was determined to be sufficient to allow the researcher to discover "rich descriptions of the participant's experiences" (Roberts and Hyatt 2019, 148).

The study adopted a purposeful criterion sampling approach to obtain publicly available and accessible documents and data to answer the research questions. The following criteria were applied when selecting the sources:

- C-suite leaders who hold leadership or management positions
- Employed by organizations headquartered in the United States
- Fluent in the English language

Nine data points from publicly available and accessible sources were used to supply the information for each research question.

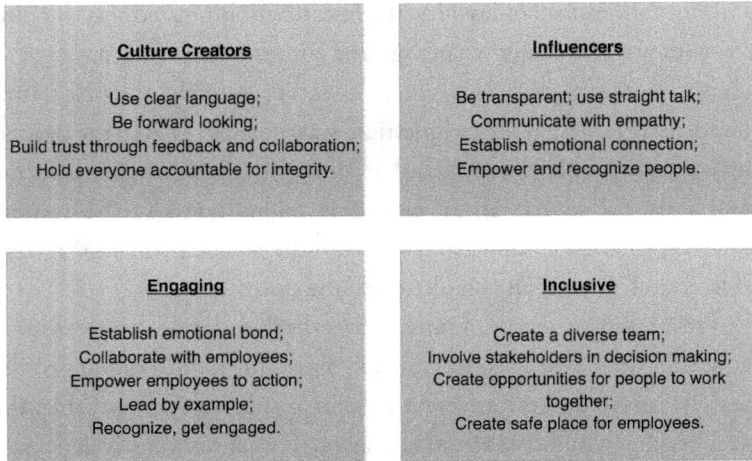

Figure 8.1. Code diagram for relational leadership strategies

Data Analysis

The following steps were utilized for data analysis following Creswell and Creswell's (2018) five-step model: (1) organize and prepare the data for analysis; (2) read and review all the data; (3) code the data; (4) generate descriptions and themes; and (5) represent the description and themes.

A deductive approach was applied during the data coding, "testing or verifying a theory rather than developing it" (Creswell and Creswell 2018, 56). A code diagram was created to assist the researcher in demonstrating which codes were identified for each theme (see Figure 8.1).

The inductive coding approach was also utilized to engage in "building from the data to broaden themes to generalized model or theory" (Creswell and Creswell 2018, 63). These categories developed into broader themes, which Braun and Clarke (2006) called recurring patterns across a data set, grouped around a central idea. Theme definitions were created based on the data content obtained through research. However, in some cases, the researcher formed the definitions based on the literature review while balancing them with the interpretation of the data content. While the most obtained data touched on four central themes for relational leaders, not all leaders offered specific strategies. For this study, the criteria for significant themes were met when most content from the websites supported data for the themes.

Methods for Verification and Trustworthiness

As discussed previously, multiple publicly available and accessible sources were utilized to substantiate the consistency of the findings. Triangulating the evidence gleaned from different data sources added a layer of credibility to the research. To establish the dependability of the identified themes, a second reviewer was utilized to independently examine the responses for consistency using the same coding process as the researcher. The term *coding* refers to the process of allocating codes, words, or phrases to denote the topics or issues addressed in segments of the data and structuring the data in a manner conducive to subsequent analysis. The interreviewer was well-versed in leadership theories, how to conduct qualitative research studies, and the data coding process. Hyatt's (2017) 10-step process was applied to establish interreviewer dependability and support the trustworthiness of this study.

1. The primary researcher analyzed the data and then met with the second reviewer to review the coding process.
2. The primary researcher selected a transcript to familiarize the reviewer with the coding process.
3. The researcher maintained the highlighted, analyzed version of the transcript.
4. The second reviewer received a clean (noncoded) copy of the selected transcript.
5. Before analysis, the researcher and reviewer read the transcript to familiarize the reviewer with the data from the transcripts and answer any questions.
6. The researcher assisted the reviewer in analyzing one selected transcript by reading the text, deciphering the general idea, assessing the fit for the research question, and identifying a relevant and appropriate theme.

7. The researcher and reviewer engaged in the coding process independently from each other, utilizing the collectively completed transcript as a guide to increase coding consistency among coders. The researcher created an interreviewer comparison sheet on a shared Excel sheet. The codes were entered under the researcher's and reviewer's separate columns.

8. The additional reviewer applied the same process to the remaining transcripts independently of the primary researcher.

9. After completing all transcripts, the primary researcher and reviewer reconvened and reviewed identified findings, discussed differences, and agreed on the conclusions. Conclusions of agreement or disagreement between the researcher and reviewer were entered into the right column. In case of a dissent, agreed-upon codes were finalized and entered in the last column of the document.

10. Criteria for significant themes were agreed upon when most participants provided supportive data.

Figure 8.2 shows an example of interreviewer collaboration through the coding process.

Following these interreviewer discussions, to promote the transparency of the coding process and increase the trustworthiness of the analysis, the transcripts' intercoder reliability (ICR) was calculated. "ICR is a numerical measure of the agreement between different coders regarding how the same data should be coded" (O'Connor and Joffe 2020, 2). While there are several ways of calculating ICR, the most common method is simply reporting the percentage of data units the coders agree (O'Connor and Joffe 2020). While there is no universally agreed-upon threshold for what is considered an acceptable ICR percentage, Landis and Koch (1977) recommended the agreement between coders to be measured through ICR percentages as follows: slight agreement when between 0 and 0.20, fair between 0.21 and 0.40, moderate between 0.41 and 0.60, substantial between 0.61 and 0.79, and perfect agreement between 0.80 and 1.

After the researcher and the secondary coder reviewed the data together and compared their analyses, the themes were agreed upon and

Leader	Primary coder	Second coder	Agreement	Disagreement	Final subtheme
A1	Intentional	Intentional	1		Intentional
A2	Forward looking	Focus		1	Forward looking
A3	Lead with integrity	Accountability		1	Lead with Integrity
A4	Reputation and trust	Reputation and trust	1		Reputation and trust
A5	Focus	Focus	1		Focus
A6	Accountability	Culture		1	Culture
A7	Obtain feedback	Obtain feedback	1		Obtain feedback
A8	Trust and collaboration	Teamwork		1	Trust and collaboration
A9	Transparency	Transparency	1		Transparency

Figure 8.2 Interviewer comparison sheet

finalized. Subsequently, the ICR rate for the entire transcript increased to 0.81, further increasing the reliability and trustworthiness of the coding process.

Reflection on Bias

Because qualitative research is interpretive exploration, where the researcher is typically involved in a sustained and intensive data review, such involvement may introduce a range of potential personal biases (Locke et al. 2013). With these concerns in mind, researchers need to identify and clearly state their "biases, values, and personal background … that shape their interpretations formed during a study" (Creswell and Creswell 2018, 182). Given that the study that shaped this book aimed to investigate the relational leadership practices employed by leaders, it is noteworthy that the researchers' interest in the subject matter may have potentially influenced the interpretations of the gathered data.

To address potential biases in research, Creswell (2018) advocated for an ongoing self-examination by researchers throughout the research process, focusing on their connection to the study's topic. To mitigate the risk of bias stemming from the researcher's interest in the subject matter and to ensure objective data interpretation, the framework for reflexivity proposed by Srivastava and Hopwood (2009) was adopted. The process involved three steps: (a) What does the data tell the researcher?—to sharpen the objective focus; (b) What does the researcher want to know?—to refine the point of interest; (c) What is the dialectical relationship between what the data is showing and what the researcher wants to know?—to identify a potential bias (Srivastava and Hopwood 2009). Furthermore, the research committee actively reviewed the data and scrutinized the researcher's findings, analysis, and conclusions.

It is essential to highlight that the significance academic research assigns to self-reflection in the research process parallels Senge's (1990) discourse on leaders' responsibility to challenge individual and organizational mental models. Consequently, methodical and deliberate self-evaluation was employed throughout the research endeavor. Moreover, a continuous reflective process and analysis were seamlessly integrated at various stages of the research process. Detailed notes taken during the data collection phase were meticulously preserved and evaluated over several months to ensure that personal experiences did not unduly influence the interpretation of the data. The final test, as always, will be the reader's interpretation and reactions to this book, which is welcomed to activate additional discourse on the subject matter so that we can continue the practice of being reflective practitioners together. This emphasis on ongoing reflection aligns with the methodical and thoughtful self-evaluation employed throughout the research process, as highlighted earlier.

Operational Definitions

- *CEO*: The CEO is a chief executive officer—the title represents the highest-ranking person in an institution, ultimately responsible for making managerial decisions and setting the course for the organization (Dewar et al. 2020; Katz and Miller 2014).
- *Charismatic leadership:* Charismatic leadership is a style in which leaders possess an extraordinary gift, enabling them to have profound and exceptional effects on followers (Antonakis 2012; Friedrich 1961; House 1976; Tucker 1968; Weber 1947).
- *Coordination of action:* Coordination of action is a social process in which the leader's voice is one among many, and the responsibility for enacting relational processes is equally distributed among leaders and followers (Brown and Hosking 1986; Dachler and Hosking 1995b; Gronn 2009).

- *C-suite:* Senior leadership positions, also known as C-suite roles, typically include titles such as CEO, chief financial officer, chief operating officer, chief risk officer, chief credit officer, and chief information officer (Groysberg et al. 2011).
- *Culture creators:* Culture creators are individuals who, among other things, lead with values and inspire others around them, leaders and followers alike, to help each other advance to a higher level of motivation (Antonakis 2012; Bass 1985, 1999; Burns 1978; Greenleaf 1977; Hollander 1992, 2010; Uhl-Bien 2006).
- *Emotional intelligence (EI):* EI is an individual's ability to perceive emotions, manage emotions, understand emotions, and facilitate using emotions (Coleman 1995; Goleman and Boyatzis 2017; Salovey and Mayer 1990).
- *Employee engagement:* Employee engagement describes the process where employees are involved in the organization's success, are enthusiastic, and committed to their work and workplace (Antonakis 2012; Carter et al. 2015; Chia 1995; Dewar et al. 2020; Fiol et al. 1999; Hosking and Pluut 2010; Katz and Miller 2014).
- *Entity perspective:* The entity perspective focuses on leadership through individual "perceptions, intentions, behaviors, personalities, expectations, and evaluations relative to their relationships with one other" (Uhl-Bien 2006, 655).
- *Executive leadership:* Executive leadership comprises senior-level managers, typically with an executive vice president or senior vice president title (Groysberg et al. 2011).
- *Inclusivity:* Inclusivity refers to the intentional, ongoing practice of diverse people being welcomed to take part in "all aspects of the work of an organization, including leadership positions and decision-making process" (Tan 2019, 31; see also Brower et al. 2000; Brown and Hosking 1986; Dachler and Hosking 1995a; Dansereau et al. 1975; Graen 2016).
- *Influencer:* Influencer refers to individuals who, in addition to strong professional and charismatic capabilities, possess high

levels of social and relational connectivity with others (Andersen and Chen 2002; Bass 1985, 1995b, 1999; Bass and Riggio 2006; Burns 1978; Friedrich 1961; House 1976; Tan 2019).

- *Leader–member exchange (LMX):* LMX describes how effective leadership relationships develop among dyad partners, such as leaders and team members or peers, to generate bases of leadership influence (Dansereau et al. 1975; Graen 2016; Lunenburg 2010; Rockstuhl 2012; Uhl-Bien 2006).

- *Leader–member, member–member (LMX-MMX):* LMX-MMX leadership moves beyond the limiting supervisor–follower relationship to outside formal reporting structures and calls for leadership sharing among various parties (Dansereau et al. 1975; Fiol et al. 1999; Graen 2016; Schyns and Day 2010).

- *Multiloguing:* Multiloguing describes the process of speaking of many, concerning many contexts in the relational perspective (Dachler and Hosking 1995a; Drath 2001).

- *Organizational culture:* Organizational culture is defined as a product and a process (Bolman and Deal 2017). "As a product, it embodies wisdom accumulated from experience" (p. 258), and, as a process, it is created and repeated by individuals who "learn the old ways and eventually become the teachers themselves" (p. 258).

- *Quality workplace environment:* A quality workplace environment where individual differences are nurtured, information is not suppressed or spun but instead openly shared with all associates, and where employees feel that the company adds value to them rather than only expecting it from them (Goffee and Jones 2013; Katz and Miller 2014; Tan 2019).

- *Relational constructionism:* Relational constructionism is a process where the leadership voice is one of many, and knowledge is discovered collectively with many parties working together (Chia 1995; Dachler and Hosking 1995b; Hosking 1988; Hosking and Pluut 2010; Uhl-Bien 2006).

- *Relational leadership:* Relational leadership style focuses on developing quality, trusting work relationships created and maintained by leaders and followers collectively (Brower et al. 2000; Graen and Uhl-Bien 1995; Hosking 1988; Hosking and Pluut 2010; Murrell 1997; Uhl-Bien 2006).

- *Relational perspective:* The relational perspective focuses on the process of relational leadership creation, where leaders and followers are collectively responsible for ultimate results (Dachler and Hosking 1995a; Hosking 1988; Uhl-Bien 2006).

- *Relational self:* Relational self stems from interpersonal relationships and interdependencies with significant others (Andersen and Chen 2002; Andersen and Glassman 1996; Baldwin et al. 1990; Baldwin and Holmes 1987).

- *Self-efficacy:* Self-efficacy is an individual's belief in self-capacity to execute behaviors necessary to produce specific performance attainments (Anderson et al. 2008; Bandura 1977, 1978; Galoji and Jibrin 2016; Judge et al. 2007; Semadar et al. 2006; Stajkovic and Luthans 1998).

- *Servant leadership:* Servant leadership is a leadership style that focuses on the well-being of the followers first, among other priorities (Avolio et al. 2009; Block 2006; Coetzer et al. 2017; Greenleaf 1977; Patterson 2003; Russell and Stone 2002; Spears 2010; Van Dierendonck 2011).

- *Social identity:* Social identity is the concept that theorizes how people see themselves within a group context (Berscheid and Reis 1998; Brewer and Gardner 1996; Hogg 2001; Smith and Henry 1996; Tajfel 1972).

- *Social network theory:* Social network theory refers to how social networks influence leaders within organizations (Balkundi and Kilduff 2005; Carter et al. 2015; Lord and Emrich 2001; Uhl-Bien 2006).

- *Transformational leadership:* Transformational leadership is a process in which leaders and followers help each other advance to a higher level of motivation and morality (Bass 1985, 1999; Bass and Riggio 2006; Burns 1978; Hollander 1992).

- *VUCA:* Volatile, uncertain, complex, ambiguous business environment.

CHAPTER 9

Relational Practices

In today's VUCA marketplace, effective leadership is crucial. Understanding the strategies that relational leaders use to shape organizational culture and leverage their influence is key to thriving in such an environment. By examining these study findings, we seek to identify how relational leaders inspire, guide, and foster a relational environment.

Our data analysis uncovered 70 total themes, captured in Figure 9.1, distributed across four central categories: relational leaders as culture creators, influencers, inclusive, and engaging. These themes reveal diverse relational strategies used by contemporary leader–practitioners, providing unique insights into their success in each thematic area. Interestingly, many of these strategies, discussed in detail later in Chapter 10, are interconnected and simultaneously influence multiple areas of relational leadership. This synergy between relational strategies can help contemporary leaders understand how relational strategies shape organizational culture to thrive in today's VUCA marketplace.

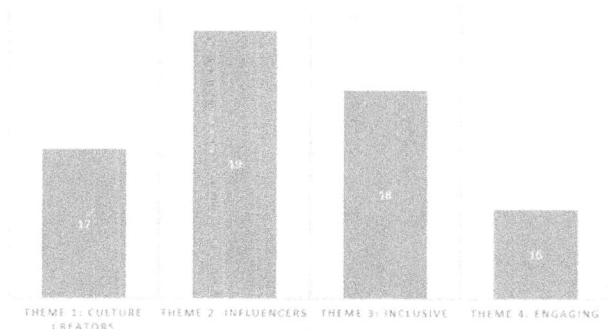

Figure 9.1 Number of initial themes for each research question

Research Question 1 and Corresponding Data

Research Question 1 was: What relational leadership strategies are commonly practiced by leaders to create quality organizational cultures? This research question correlates to the theme of relational leaders as culture creators. Culture creators are defined as those who lead with values and inspire others around them, leaders and followers alike, to help each other advance to a higher level of motivation (Antonakis 2012; Bass 1985, 1999; Burns 1978; Greenleaf 1977; Hollander 1992, 2010; Uhl-Bien 2006). While 100 percent of the data points addressed the theme of culture creators, most of the leaders (six out of nine) offered specific strategies for culture creation. Here are some responses that were captured in this category.

- Leaders need to be intentional about the type of culture they want to build. If you do not worry about the culture, you will still have one. It will be an unintentional culture. We did an employee survey and found ten indicators of our highly unintentional culture—examples like "dump-and-blame" culture or "hair on fire" management. We had to regroup and define what culture we wanted to build (A1).
- We asked leaders to use clear language to set the expectations on the type of culture we wanted to have and provide clear examples. The key to our leadership model is simplicity: You can read one of two paragraphs of information and clearly know what we are asking for. It must be simple and to the point (A2).
- Companies are evaluated based on their financial performance, reported quarterly earnings, and the impact of words CEOs' statements on market movements. However, wouldn't it be even better if the market trusts these companies because of their commitment to having a culture that is committed to ethical practices? Such a culture would ensure the company's longevity not just for the next quarter or a year but for the next decade and beyond (A3).
- Translating the corporate culture into internal practice starts with the leader. After gaining a comprehensive overview of a

particular business line or initiative, I like to immerse myself in the trenches—frequently visiting different departments to talk to employees. Every few months, I provide them with a direct line of communication, ensuring I keep my ear to the ground. Through this practice, I have discovered the importance of granting employees greater freedom to serve customers better. We must have a culture where it is OK to make mistakes (A7).

- Traditionally, our culture was based on expertise and products, but the landscape is changing quickly. Our culture must adapt. We involved 700 employees in the process. Employees who enjoy a positive, supportive work culture will, in turn, transmit positivity to their customers. Improving the methods and tools for continuous employee feedback is the key to our cultural transformation and continuity (A8).
- I believe it's crucial for individuals to have access to and comprehend the organization's focus and priorities.
- I think it is important that people can access and understand where the focus and priorities are. When you have a stable organization, it is important to step back and evaluate if the culture still makes sense, particularly in a changing environment. The key is to have strategic clarity, starting with articulating the purpose of the organization (A9).

Several noteworthy patterns emerged when reviewing the data content. There were 17 original subthemes recognized between the researcher and the interreviewer derived from the nine sources identified for the first research question. There were four significant subtheme categories where the majority of the data mapped into (a) use straightforward language to articulate culture (four subthemes), (b) be forward-looking when setting the culture (four subthemes), (c) build trust with stakeholders through feedback and collaboration (four subthemes), and (d) integrity (two subthemes) (Figure 9.2).

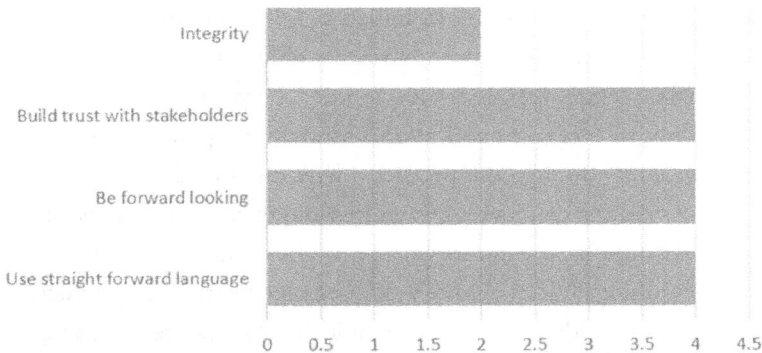

Figure 9.2 Summary of the subthemes generated from RQ1

Research Question 2 and Corresponding Data

Research Question 2 was: What relational leadership strategies are commonly practiced by leaders to influence others? This research question correlates to the theme of relational leaders as influencers. Influencers are defined as those who, in addition to strong professional and charismatic capabilities, possess high levels of social and relational connectivity with others (Andersen & Chen 2002; Bass 1985, 1995b, 1999; Bass & Riggio 2006; Burns 1978; Friedrich 1961; House 1976; Tan 2019). While 100 percent of the data points addressed the theme of influence, most leaders offered specific strategies to influence others. Here are some examples of the data that were captured in this category.

- I don't like corporate talk. I value straightforward communication. Transparency and authenticity are important. In my opinion, empathy is the way to bridge everything. I have learned the courage to talk straight, but if you do it with empathy, you can be a straight talker without being an unpleasant person (B1).
- Creating connections with people is how you create value for employees and customers (B2).
- He is not a grand gesturing, back-slapping leader, but rather, he works in subtle ways behind the scenes to make sure people understand the needs of the organization. He always stays in the shadows, like the Wizard of Oz, pulling the cords and the

buttons, but there is no question that he cares deeply about the people in the organization. What you see is what you get with him (B3).

- Meetings are focused on deepening the emotional connection between the team members. The enemy is not the other person, but the negativity when sometimes communication is broken when the dialogue is not occurring. We do not, in corporate America, slow down enough to realize what triggers us and how that influences how we think, feel, and the way we look at the person in front of us (B4).

- It is easy to talk a good game, but people follow what they see and not what they hear. Leading by example is the best way to lead (B5).

- I have been very visible about asking for feedback. Even with tough feedback, I remain positive so people do not feel we will ever shoot the messenger. We need to be more direct in talking with one another, use clear language, and be patience in hearing feedback. It puts people at ease to speak with you (B6).

- Candor is critical in forming relationships and influencing others. It is a false kindness when you do not tell people where they stand or do not share the full picture. However, you have got to do it with empathy. People respect candor (B8).

Several notable patterns became apparent upon reviewing the data content. Nineteen subthemes from a total of nine sources were identified. The significant subtheme categories related to the theme of Influencers that emerged in the research were (a) empathy (five subthemes), (b) emotional connection (four subthemes), (c) transparency and honesty (four subthemes), and (d) straight talk (three subthemes) (Figure 9.3).

Research Question 3 and Corresponding Data

Research Question 3 was: What relational leadership strategies are commonly practiced by leaders to create inclusivity? This research question correlates to the theme of relational leaders as inclusive.

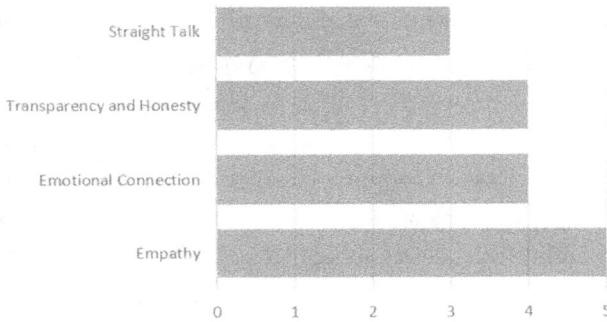

Figure 9.3 Summary of the subthemes generated from RQ2

Inclusivity refers to the intentional, ongoing practice of diverse people being welcomed to take part in all aspects of the work of an organization, including leadership positions and the decision-making process (Tan 2019, 31; see also Brower et al. 2000; Brown and Hosking 1986; Dachler and Hosking 1995a; Dansereau et al. 1975; Graen 2016). 100 percent of the data points addressed the theme of inclusivity and offered specific strategies for building inclusive organizational cultures. Here are some examples of the data that were captured in this category.

- It makes you appreciate how different people with different ideas and backgrounds can come together and create great things together. With that diversity, you are a lot better off, a lot stronger, and more innovative than if you were all cut out of the same mold. Leaders need to find ways to create such environments. (C1)
- Selfishly, you need to get feedback from every possible source—in every way you can: Survey Monkey, group meetings with employees, one-on-one meetings, and client feedback. Employees know best what the issues are with the company or a particular situation. To get the best feedback, you have to surround yourself with diverse talent and allow everyone to be heard. (C2)
- You must have a culture where there is no special club or a special class of citizens in the workplace. You need to have a

culture where you are not only treated with respect but also able to speak up. (C3)

- We believe that achieving strong operating results starts with our employee team, which must reflect the diversity of the clients and communities we serve. Our diversity makes us stronger, and the value we deliver as a company is strengthened when we bring broad perspectives together to meet the needs of our diverse stakeholders. It starts from the top; leaders set the tone. (C4)

- It all starts with people. There has been a shift in our organization in growing talent and pulling them through. This internal mobility is a big focus for us. Things do not happen overnight. It is a long-term approach, as it takes a long time to develop people. And it is a team approach. To develop people, it takes more than one person, one mentor, and one coach. But this approach is rewarded by people feeling belonging and included. (C5)

- Developing a positive workplace has been instrumental in our organization. Our team did a lot to define our culture here, and they came up with five cultural cornerstones we live by today. The first and most important one is "better together." We all really believe that means something in our company. Together is a keyword here. (C6)

- The nation's changing demographics are an amazing force for good. The goal is to integrate various voices and minds in solving problems. It has to be purposeful, coordinated, and all working toward the same objectives. (C7)

- Diversity is a fact; inclusion is a choice. The board remains committed to increasing the representation of women in leadership positions. The company's voluntary goals for female representation remain unchanged and focus on the top three corporate titles (in headcount terms): managing director, director, and vice president. These goals form part of the key performance indicators on the "Balanced Scorecard" for the organization. (C8)

- Inclusivity is not just with employees but also with clients. Everything we do is inspired by our clients. We adapt to their experiences and adjust to their lifestyles. (C9)

Upon reviewing the data content, several significant patterns were observed. Eighteen subthemes from a total of nine sources were identified. The significant subtheme categories related to the theme of Inclusive that emerged in the research were (a) create a diverse team (five subthemes), (b) teamwork (four subthemes), (c) create a safe environment for employees (four subthemes), and (d) employee development (two subthemes) (Figure 9.4).

Research Question 4 and Corresponding Data

Research Question 4 was: What relational leadership strategies are commonly practiced by leaders to create employee and organizational engagement? This research question correlates to the theme of relational leaders as engaging. Engagement describes the process where employees are involved in the organization's success, are enthusiastic, and committed to their work and workplace (Antonakis 2012; Carter et al. 2015; Chia 1995; Dewar et al. 2020; Fiol et al. 1999; Hosking and Pluut 2010; Katz and Miller 2014). 100 percent of the data points addressed the engagement theme and offered specific strategies for building an engaging culture in their organizations. Here are some examples of the data that were captured in this category.

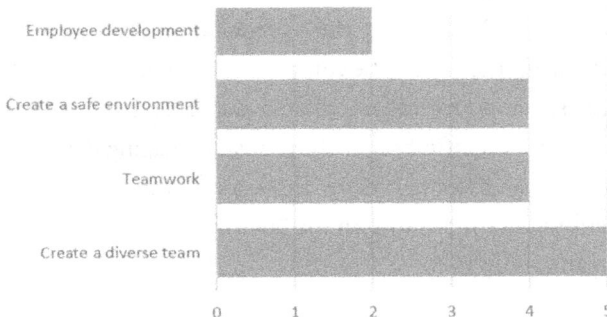

Figure 9.4 Summary of the subthemes generated from RQ3

- Employers are desperate for engagement and loyalty from their employees. We must ask ourselves: What is that magic ingredient that creates loyalty and engagement from employees? The answer is experience; People want experience from their employers and their leaders. They want more than just a salary. So, the question we as leaders need to ask ourselves when making decisions is how this particular decision impacts employees and their experience with their leader and the organization (D1).

- We listen, the management team is open. Our agenda is set by employees. If you work for me, I expect you to raise every-thing that's important, everything and anything, bureaucracies, challenges... and so on (D2).

- We have newly hired younger talent and highly valued seasoned colleagues in the organization. What makes our secret source the best in class is the collaboration between these groups and between them and the management team. We still have some bonding to do as an organization—it takes more discussion and focus (D3).

- Companies often talk about doing one thing or another to increase employee engagement. However, the question is never asked about what employees can do to get engaged. When JFK said, "Ask not what your country can do for you, but what you can do for your country," the framework for engagement changed to personal accountability. Similarly, the leader's role in engaging employees is to create an environment where employees take responsibility to get engaged (D4).

- People need to have fun. Help people to get excited about what they are doing, create an enjoyable work environment, have fun, and then recognize them publicly with great fanfare for a job well done. When people are not having fun and are not recognized, and no one says thanks, they become disengaged and feel unimportant. Recognition is corporate America's most underutilized tool. It is more important than compensation and benefits (D5).

- Stress can get to you, and others can see it. One thing I could not do was to let my team see how concerned I was during stressful situations. And they never knew. During stressful situations, you are alone, by yourself, trying to stay focused. During stressful situations, I communicate five to six times a day so that people are informed, they know I do not trick them, and they know where I stand and where they stand (D6).
- Be transparent, open, fact-based, and treat people with respect, but also have high requirements for people to deliver. It's important that they trust you. You can be firm but fair (D7).
- The company is now unrelenting on its cultural values, ensuring that management leads by example. These values were recently redefined and simplified to "fun, family, and empowerment." This has included encouraging and supporting staff to grow personally and professionally. Our staff is my number one priority: Happy staff, happy clients (D8).
- Success is to create a culture where people say—I enjoy working here. Any organization's success depends on the team and how they pull together. I keep saying this to my team, and it has become our motto. Employees know that if someone has an issue, they are in a family environment, and people help each other (D9).

Upon reviewing the data content, numerous notable patterns surfaced, identifying 16 subthemes from a total of nine sources. The significant subtheme categories related to the theme of Engagers

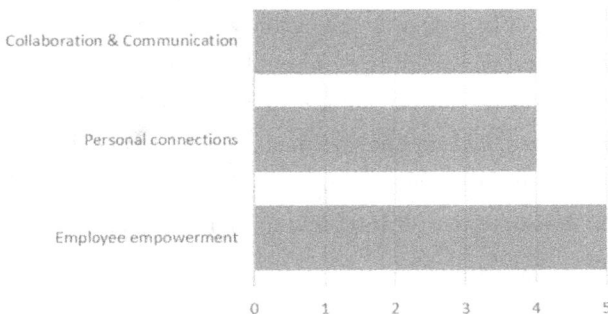

Figure 9.5 Summary of the subthemes generated from RQ4

Table 9.1 Research questions and significant subthemes

Theme	Research question	Subthemes
Culture creators	RQ1: What relational leadership strategies are commonly practiced by executives to create high-quality organizational cultures?	• Use clear language to articulate culture • Be forward-looking when setting the culture • Build trust with stakeholders through feedback and collaboration • Hold everyone accountable for integrity
Influencer	RQ2: What relational leadership strategies are commonly practiced by executives to influence others?	• Communicate with empathy • Establish an emotional connection with employees • Transparency and honesty • Use straight talk
Inclusive	RQ3: What relational leadership strategies are commonly practiced by executives to create inclusivity?	• Create a diverse team • Teamwork • Create a safe environment for employees • Employee development
Engaging	RQ4: What relational leadership strategies are commonly practiced by executives to create high employee and organizational engagement?	• Employee empowerment • Personal connection • Collaboration and communication

that emerged in the research were (a) employee empowerment (five subthemes), (b) personal connections (four subthemes), and (c) collaboration and communication (four subthemes) (Figure 9.5).

Table 9.1 summarizes significant subthemes uncovered from the data content related to each research question.

CHAPTER 10

Leading Together

Dr. Stephen R. Covey once famously said to begin with the end in mind. With that wisdom, let's revisit the two primary objectives of this book. First, it aimed to investigate the existence of a tangible connection between relational leadership theory and its practical application in real-world contexts. Second, it sought to explore the relational strategies employed by real-life leaders to cultivate quality workplace environments.

In the previous nine chapters, we've embarked on an extensive journey, exploring the relational leadership theory and understanding how relational leaders create inclusive and engaging organizational cultures that thrive in VUCA environments. Building on a solid theoretical foundation, we thoroughly investigated various relational leadership models and identified central themes for relational leadership. We then designed and conducted a research study to examine how leaders apply relational leadership in real-life situations. Finally, we obtained credible data from leader practitioners on specific words and actions they use to build positive organizational cultures, engage stakeholders, and create inclusive workplace environments that enable both the organization and its people to thrive together. The final task remains to analyze the data we obtained, glean some actionable ideas that leaders could use for creating quality workplace environments, and validate these conclusions by comparing them with the relational leadership theory.

A close analysis of the research data revealed 14 critical practices relational leaders use to create quality workplace environments. These emergent themes highlight a clear and direct connection between the strategies practicing relational leaders use to establish quality workplace environments and the theoretical framework of relational leadership.

Consistent with the entity perspective of relational leadership theory, which focuses on leaders' actions, the study identified several essential practices that underscore the importance of a leader's personal style: straight talk, being forward-looking, emotional connection, transparency, honesty, and empathy. These practices focus on relationship building from the individual perspective, with the leader as a focal point. Alternatively, consistent with the relational perspective, the study revealed several leadership practices demonstrating how leaders shift their focus to a collective or shared leadership dynamic. These practices included building diverse teams to foster a rich feedback loop, creating a safe space for employees to speak up, encouraging teamwork and collaboration, and establishing trust with stakeholders through reciprocal feedback.

Synthesizing these contrasting approaches, we can conclude that relational leaders begin building a quality workplace environment by first implementing individual strategies aligned with the entity perspective. However, to institute sustainable engagement and cultivate a lasting workplace culture, they shift their focus toward involving all stakeholders in every aspect of the leadership process. According to the theoretical model, authentic relational leadership is achieved by integrating practices from both perspectives, creating a synergy between these distinct approaches to create high-quality workplace environments.

Interestingly, upon closer inspection of the original findings, some notable patterns emerged that resonated with the relational leadership's theoretical model that seamlessly incorporates both entitative and relational perspectives. For instance, establishing personal emotional connections with stakeholders emerges as a common subtheme in both categories of relational practice: influencing and engaging others. Similarly, the subtheme of using straight talk, characterized by clear and direct communication, correlates with relational leaders as culture creators and influencers. The original 14 relational practices were distilled into 12 by consolidating these subthemes across multiple thematic areas, as highlighted in Table 10.1. This synthesis reinforces that certain relational practices possess versatility in their impact on

Table 10.1 Practices demonstrated by relational leaders creating quality workplace environments

Culture creators	Influencers	Inclusive	Engaging
Straight talk	Empathy	Create diverse team	Empowerment
Forward-looking	Emotional connection	Teamwork	Personal connections
Build trust through feedback and collaboration	Transparency and honesty	Create safe environment	Communication and collaboration
	Straight talk	Develop people	

building quality workplace environments. These practices can simultaneously influence various aspects of the workplace environment, serving as valuable tools for leaders seeking to foster positive and enduring organizational environments.

A further examination of the 4 central themes and 12 associated practices for creating quality workplace environments revealed compelling insights about relational leaders. Consistent with the theoretical model, it is important to reemphasize that these observations should not be considered in isolation. Instead, as you will see, these strategies are interconnected and work in unison, creating a unified approach that strengthens relational leadership and cultivates a thriving organizational culture. Let's delve into this analysis together.

Relational Leaders as Culture Creators

What was unequivocally clear from the research was that relational leaders are primarily and fundamentally culture creators. Their approach to leadership reflects a zeal-like commitment to shaping and nurturing organizational culture, rooted in the unwavering focus on the future. Like custodians of a sacred mission, they are driven by a profound sense of purpose, continuously striving to forge a culture that echoes the organization's present values and reflects the aspirations for meeting future opportunities and challenges.

While it may not come as a shock that fostering a culture is a crucial trait of effective leadership, what sets relational leaders apart is their unique approach to executing this strategy. Relational leaders transcend superficial corporate rhetoric about the importance of organizational culture by prioritizing trust-building above anything. Their commitment to trust-building goes beyond token corporate gestures and is deeply ingrained in a nuanced approach to every action they take. Such a deliberate and authentic personal approach fosters an environment of unity, purpose, and shared values in their organizations, creating a sustainable culture of engagement.

When it comes to trust-building, relational leaders do not leave anyone behind. One of the data excerpts revealed: You must have a culture where there is no special club or a special class of citizens in the workplace. This sentiment aligns with the LMX theory proposed by Dansereau et al. (1975), which contends that leaders who understand the significance of LMX recognize that they need to avoid creating out-groups wherever possible and maximize the size of the in-group. Studies show that fostering high-quality LMX results in enhanced organizational commitment, improved job attitudes, and greater employee engagement—key elements that ultimately define the success of organizational culture (Beverly 2016; Gajendran and Aparna 2012; Graen 2016; Lunenburg 2010; Power 2013; Rockstuhl 2012).

Relational Leaders as Influencers

Relational leaders have a remarkable ability to influence people. While a common interpretation of the word *influence* in an organizational setting may suggest the use of corporate titles and their inherent power, what emerges as particularly fascinating is the relational leaders' reliance on genuine empathy as the cornerstone of their influence. While the theme of empathy resonates throughout the dataset, one specific excerpt from the data encapsulates this phenomenon perfectly:

> I do not like corporate talk. I value straightforward communication. Transparency and authenticity are paramount. In my view, empathy serves as the bridge to everything. While I have learned to speak frankly, it is when empathy guides my words that I can be direct without coming across as harsh or unkind.

Relational leaders recognize that empathetic communication fosters trust, nurtures understanding, and forges an emotional connection with their followers—a subtheme that resonated strongly in the data. One of the leaders expressed: Creating connections with people is how you create value for employees and customers. Another leader stated: Meetings are focused on deepening emotional connection between the team members. The benefits of establishing emotional connections with employees and leading effectively—a concept that Goleman (1998) called EI—are well documented in leadership theory. Salovey and Mayer (1990) described EI as the individual's ability to perceive, manage, understand, and facilitate using emotions. Goleman (1998) claimed that most effective leaders have one thing in common, "they have a high degree of what has come to be known as emotional intelligence" (p. 1).

It is important to emphasize here that these emotional connections are not insignificant. They are established through genuine care for people. Such an authentic, empathetic approach equips relational leaders to navigate intricate situations with their followers with trust and compassion, empowering them to positively influence others for the betterment of the organization. To underscore the critical importance of these findings, let's examine a real-life situation that highlights the consequences when leaders fail to navigate sensitive situations with empathy and care for their followers.

I recently spoke with an executive of a multi-billion-dollar company acquired recently by a larger institution. He shared some of the painful challenges he and his leadership team were experiencing as they adapted to the new organization's culture and the styles of the new executive team. While changes caused by mergers are inevitable and often necessary, there is a period during the merger process when employees anxiously await news about which positions may be eliminated and who will stay or leave. Employees often have fundamental concerns during this time: Does the new organization understand my value? Am I safe? Are my direct reports safe? While some of this anxiety may be unavoidable, it is typically a period when leaders and followers alike operate with fear and low levels of trust. Although these situations could be breakthrough moments for building trust and transparency within the organization, most executives could handle this process better. When an organization operates under the cloak of the unknown and fear, the longer this period lasts without transparent and empathetic communication, the greater the pain and the deeper the scars of distrust after everything settles.

Despite being a seasoned professional with a successful track record of adapting to ever-changing organizational processes and culture, the executive I spoke with shared these concerns. The most striking moment in our discussion was a situation he painfully recounted when his new boss called him on a Tuesday and asked to meet early Friday morning.

When the executive asked if he should prepare anything, his boss said it wasn't necessary, and he just wanted a conversation. Given the timing, which coincided with layoff announcements, the executive naturally assumed he was about to be fired. He went home and told his wife he would likely lose his job on Friday.

The executive shared that the most difficult part wasn't the thought of him losing his job but the 3-day wait to hear the news. He painfully recounted that his mind was so consumed with the upcoming news that he was not mentally or emotionally present for his team at work or his family at home. When Friday came, he arrived at the office earlier than usual and found his boss already there. Inviting him into the office, his boss started a regular conversation, asking him about various financial standings and general business trends. After some time, the boss finally revealed he was planning to go on vacation and wanted the executive to oversee specific areas of the business operation in his absence. The executive agreed to help but then asked his boss if he realized the heartache he had caused over the last 3 days. Given the layoffs and the abrupt meeting request, he explained what he had assumed and asked if his boss understood the impact of his communication. The boss was apologetic, admitting that he was so overwhelmed with the newly combined organization and the potential of missing important deadlines while on vacation that he completely missed his request's effect on the executive. In other words, the executive's boss shared that he was also highly stressed. He added that he wanted to ask for the executive's help during his absence precisely because he valued the executive's leadership and needed his support.

OK, maybe he corrected the mistake in the end, and after all, who among us hasn't made one? Yet, this is a perfect example of what happens when leaders operate without empathy. If the executive's boss put his direct report at the forefront of his thoughts and recognized the sensitivity of the situation and the importance of transparent and empathetic communication, he could have used this opportunity to forge a stronger personal and emotional connection with him by simply saying: "Let's meet this Friday in your office. I recognize these are stressful times in the organization, but please don't be alarmed. I want to meet because I plan to go on vacation, and considering the changes we're going through, I'm relying on your leadership and support to handle certain things while I'm away. I greatly value you and your effectiveness in the organization, and I look forward to discussing how we can work closely together to help our company through these changes." By communicating with such empathy and transparency, the executive's boss could have eliminated unnecessary stress, allowing his direct report to remain effective and focused on work and homelife. What a missed opportunity!

Unfortunately, this isn't an isolated incident; similar situations occur daily across organizations, leading to significant adverse impacts. The root cause of such issues is not a lack of communication or an inability to express thoughts effectively; it is a lack of empathy and the failure to consider others' feelings and thoughts in every decision—something that relational leaders inherently understand and prioritize. By placing empathy at the core of their leadership approach, relational leaders effortlessly build an authentic trust, which is essential for genuine mutual influence between relational leaders and their followers. In return, this dynamic foster genuine collaboration and cultivates an engaging culture that rewards the organization and its people.

Relational Leaders as Inclusive

The third prominent theme characterizing relational leaders is their profound dedication to inclusivity, which they notably accomplish by building highly diverse teams. *Diversity is a fact, and inclusion is a choice* —stated one leader. For relational leaders, promoting diversity in their organizations is not just a catchphrase used for corporate branding but rather the main ingredient in their modus operandi. Relational leaders deliberately cultivate diversity within their organizations because they recognize the significant value of diverse perspectives in sound decision making. They firmly believe optimal outcomes can only be achieved in an environment where individuals feel respected and empowered to voice their opinions. This approach, in turn, enables them to create a positive and engaging organizational culture, which is, once again, a fundamental priority for relational leaders. One executive stated:

It makes you appreciate how different people with different ideas and backgrounds can come together and create great things together. With that diversity, you are a lot better off, a lot stronger, and more innovative than if you were all cut out of the same mold. Leaders need to find ways to create such environments.

Furthermore, inclusive relational leaders are enthusiastic about people development and passionately committed to fostering teamwork. They don't depend on the transactional aspect of their relationships with followers, expecting value merely because of compensation. Instead, relational leaders actively engage with and support their team members' professional and personal development, recognizing that developing people takes time and sustained organizational effort. One of the researched leaders said:

> Our organization has shifted toward growing talent and retaining them. Internal mobility is a big focus for us. Things do not happen overnight; it is a long-term approach.

Such profound organizational pledge to employee development enables relational leaders to cultivate an environment where followers feel a sense of commitment from their executives, motivating them to give their best back to their leaders and their organization. Consequently, all stakeholders—leaders, employees, the organization, and its clients—benefit from such an inclusive environment.

Relational Leaders as Engaging

The fourth notable characteristic of relational leaders is their exceptional ability to engage followers. While conventional leadership may assume that follower engagement with leaders naturally arises because of leaders' corporate titles, professional expertise, or employees' monetary compensation, relational leaders intuitively understand that authentic engagement stems from establishing genuine, mutual, personal connections and creating positive experiences with those around them.

It is striking that the theme of forging personal connections and the value of individual attention emerges repeatedly throughout the dataset, powerfully reinforcing the idea that the relational leadership strategies identified in the study profoundly impact cultivating a quality workplace environment. A statement one of the leaders shared emphasizes this approach:

> Employers are desperate for engagement and loyalty from their employees. We must ask ourselves: What is that magic ingredient that creates loyalty and engagement from employees? The answer is experience. People want experience from their employers and their leaders. They want more than just a salary. So, the question we as leaders need to ask ourselves when making decisions is how this decision impacts employees and their experience with their leader and the organization.

The statement above resonates with a sentiment often heard in organizations with high employee turnover: people don't leave companies; they leave their bosses. Alternatively, leaders who build personal connections and positive experiences with their employees are rewarded with followers who become their raving fans. Through their connection with the leader, these followers become highly engaged stakeholders.

The researched data also revealed the concepts of social constructionism captured in the theoretical review. In Chapter 6, relational constructionism was defined as a process where the leadership voice is one of many, and knowledge is discovered collectively with many parties working together (Chia 1995; Dachler and Hosking 1995b; Hosking 1988; Hosking and Pluut 2010; Uhl-Bien 2006). Simply put, organizations where all stakeholders, regardless of their roles and titles, genuinely have a say in shaping the company's culture tend to be more cohesive, resilient, and successful. Grint (2005) claimed that leaders are not individual agents, able to manipulate the world around them, but rather part of the reality they create with other stakeholders involved in the process. Understanding that giving employees a voice is not the same as conducting 360-degree feedback sessions, where leaders receive candid but anonymous feedback. Nor is it when leaders ask for opinions on various topics, merely hoping to gather additional data or, worse, to create the illusion that employee feedback matters. Contrary to these illusionary behaviors that only pretend to have a culture of feedback, the authentic leadership voice of many occurs only in such environments where all stakeholders feel a genuine personal obligation to provide unsolicited, candid feedback to each other for mutual improvement. These environments do not emerge magically. They require systematic and methodical building, and while leaders must initiate the creation of such spaces, the ultimate construction of such cultures is possible only through a strong engagement with the entire organization. Those who will understand this concept and act accordingly are, in turn, rewarded with highly engaged stakeholders. Consistent with this approach, one of the leaders in the research stated:

> Traditionally, our culture was based on expertise and products, but the landscape is changing quickly. Our culture must adapt. We involved 700 employees in the process. Employees who enjoy a positive, supportive work culture will, in turn, transmit positivity to their customers. Improving the methods and tools for continuous employee feedback is the key to our cultural transformation and continuity.

Relational leaders prioritize building meaningful relationships with their team members, transcending hierarchical boundaries to foster an environment of trust and collaboration. This approach empowers followers to feel valued, respected, and engaged, which cultivates a sense of ownership and commitment toward their leader and organizational goals. By investing in authentic connections and actively involving their followers in the decision-making processes, relational leaders inspire greater loyalty, motivation, and productivity among their teams.

Contrarian Perspective

While the implications of these findings are compelling, it is essential to recognize that this book presents a singular viewpoint on leadership theory, particularly emphasizing the positive aspects of relational leaders as culture creators, influencers, inclusive, and engaging. Practical scholarly discourse involves acknowledging the potential limitations of the discussed theory and engaging with diverse perspectives. This approach aligns with what Senge (1990) recommended for leaders and organizations to examine mental models and challenge "the deeply held internal images of how the world works" (p. 163). As reflective practitioners, we must question our beliefs to ensure that familiar ways of thinking do not hinder our pursuit of truth. With this in mind, let's explore some drawbacks of relational leadership theory so that our readers can join in on this reflective questioning process.

One criticism of the central relational themes discussed in this chapter is that they assume all followers will favor leaders with highly personalized interactive styles. However, individuals are uniquely different, and assuming everyone desires a highly involved leader who wants to connect with them personally would be misleading. What happens if an individual with different values encounters a relational leader in the workplace? One potential negative outcome is that the individual may feel alienated and disenfranchised and ultimately leave the organization. According to the theory, this scenario would also be a loss for a relational leader who aims to ensure that no one is left behind.

Additionally, whether relational leadership models developed in Western culture can be as effective in another cultural context remains to be determined (Rockstuhl 2012). Several leadership studies in Asia suggested that leader–follower dynamics may operate differently in more collectivistic and higher power distance cultures (Power 2013; Rockstuhl 2012). For example, an exploration of the effects of group identity in Scottish and Indian business organizations demonstrated followers' propensity to favor a highly depersonalized leadership style, where leaders were recognized for practicing less favoritism and regarded as fairer and more equitable (Power 2013). Therefore, the effectiveness of relational leadership in non-Western cultures remains uncertain (Power 2013; Rockstuhl 2012).

Moreover, although the relational leadership model places high value on social constructionism in the workplace (leadership voice being one of many), there may be some unforeseen complexities in real-life situations. Within the context of this relational model, Graen (2016) argued that follower characteristics often fall between two extremes—some followers prefer extensive leadership sharing, and others prefer none. The reality is usually more complex, with individuals falling somewhere on this vast spectrum. Consequently, relational leaders would face the complicated task of accurately discerning each employee's preferred style.

Furthermore, while the theory emphasizes that a supportive and empathetic leadership atmosphere encourages all stakeholders to contribute to building a positive organizational culture, it assumes that everyone shares the same values and equally deserves each other's trust and reliance. Unfortunately, desiring a mutually beneficial leadership environment does not guarantee that leader and follower values will align. For true leader–follower alignment, all stakeholders must equally value their mutual relationship (Schyns and Day 2010), and such an utopian ideal may not be attainable in the real world.

Final Thoughts

Despite some drawbacks of the relational model, the potential benefits of using the relational leadership approach to create an enduring and thriving workplace environment are substantial. While the COVID-19 pandemic notably accelerated already strenuous leader–follower dynamics at the workplace, future disruptions could further exacerbate complexities in workplace cultures. Today's dynamic, hyper-competitive, and ever-changing business environment, which challenges every leadership approach, requires a new paradigm, "nothing less than admitting that the concept of the all-knowing, all-powerful leader is obsolete and that our entire image of leadership itself must change" (Katz and Miller 2014, 40). Leaders should continuously reassess their mental models, remaining open to new perspectives and innovative strategies for interacting with employees and cultivating organizational cultures. This involves an ongoing process of self-reflection, learning, and adaptation, where all stakeholders, regardless of their titles and organizational roles, actively explore new ways with different approaches. The fitting truism here is not "don't fix what's not broken," but rather, "fix it because it will be broken."

Today's leaders are expected to connect with those they lead, inspire them, and create "a sense of safety so that people can bring their best selves to work" (Katz and Miller 2014, 40). However, the efforts of individual leaders or even a group of executives alone cannot bring about meaningful organizational change in a VUCA environment. To thrive in such conditions, organizations must transform into cultures where employees are deeply involved in questioning, surfacing, and testing mental models while working with their leaders to build trust-based, caring, and inclusive environments. The relational strategies from the study highlighted in this book offer valuable insights for building such cultures. Companies achieving this goal will have a higher chance of creating quality workplace environments where the organization and its people thrive together.

In conclusion, leading together through relational leadership is more than just a theoretical model; it is a practical approach that can transform organizations. Relational leaders can foster environments where everyone feels valued and empowered by placing empathy, trust, transparency, teamwork, collaboration, and mutual respect at the forefront. The insights and strategies discussed in this book provide a roadmap for leaders who aspire to create resilient, inclusive, and engaging cultures. As we navigate the complexities of today's VUCA world, adopting relational leadership practices is not just beneficial but also essential. Through these practices, leaders can cultivate thriving and resilient organizational cultures, ensuring continual success and growth.

References

Aiello, M.J., and H.P. Tarbert. 2010. "Bank M&A in the Wake of Dodd-Frank. *The Banking Law Journal* 127 (10): 909–923. www.weil.com/~/media/Files/PDFs/Bank_MA_in_Wake_of_Dodd-Frank.pdf.

Allport, G.W., and H.S. Odbert. 1936. "TraitNnames: A Psycho-Lexical Study." *Psychological Monographs* 47 (211): i–171.

Andersen, S.M., and S. Chen. 2002. "The Relational Self: An Interpersonal Social-Cognitive Theory." *Psychological Review* 109 (4): 619–645. https://doi.org/10.1037/0033-295X.109.4.619.

Andersen, S.M., and N.S. Glassman. 1996. "Responding to Significant Others When They Are not There: Effects on Interpersonal Inference, Motivation, and Affect." In *Handbook of Motivation and Cognition: The Interpersonal Context*, edited by R.M. Sorrentino and E.T. Higgins, 3 vols, 262–321. The Guilford Press.

Anderson, D.W., H.T. Krajewski, R. Goffin, and D.N. Jackson. 2008. "A Leadership Self-Efficacy Taxonomy and Its Relation to Effective Leadership Behavior." *The Leadership Quarterly* 19 (5): 595–608. https://doi.org/10.1016/j.leaqua.2008.07.003.

Antonakis, J. 2012. "Transformational and Charismatic Leadership." In *The Nature of Leadership*, edited by D.V. Day and J. Antonakis, 2nd ed., 256–288. SAGE.

Avolio, B.J., E. Walumbwa, and T.J. Weber. 2009. "Leadership: Current Theories, Research and Future Directions." *ResearchGate*. https://doi.org/10.1146/annurev.psych.60.110707 163621.

Baldwin, M.W., S.E. Carrell, and D.F. Lopez. 1990. "Priming Relationship Schemes: My Advisor and Pope Are Watching Me From the Back of My Mind." *Journal of Experimental Social Psychology* 26: 434–454. https://selfesteemgames.mcgill.ca/research/JESP1990.pdf.

Baldwin, M.W., and J.G. Holmes. 1987. "Salient Private Audiences and Awareness of the Self. *Journal of Personality and Social Psychology* 52 (6): 1087–1098. file:///C:/Users/rband/Downloads/Salient_Private_Audiences_and_Awareness_of_the_Sel.pdf.

Balkundi, P., and M. Kilduff. 2005. "The Ties That Lead: A Social Network Approach to Leadership." *The Leadership Quarterly* 16 (1): 941–961. https://doi.org/10.1016/j.leaqua.2005.09.004.

Bandura, A. 1977. "Self-Efficacy: Toward a Unifying Theory of Behavioral Change." *Psychological Review* 84 (2): 191–215.

Bandura, A. 1978. "The Self System in Reciprocal Determinism." *American Psychologist* 33 (4): 344–358.

Bandura, A. n.d. "Self-Efficacy." *Stanford University*. www.uky.edu/~eushe2/Bandura/Bandura1994EHB.pdf.

Bandura, A., and F.J. Jourden. 1991. "Self-Regulatory Mechanisms Governing the Impact of Social Comparison on Complex Decision Making." *Journal of Personality and Social Psychology* 60 (6): 941–951.

Bannister, R. 2014. *The Four-Minute Mile,* 15th ed. Globe Pequot Press.

Bar-On, R. 2006. "The Bar-On Model of Emotional-Social Intelligence." *ResearchGate*. www.researchgate.net/publication/6509274.

Barrero, M., Bloom, N., & Davis, S. J. (2021).. Don't force people to come back to the office full time. *Harvard Business Review,*August 2024 https://hbr.org/2021/08/dont-force-people-to-come-back-to-the-office-full-time

Bass, B. M. (1985). *Leadership and Performance Beyond Expectations.* Free Press.

Bass, B. M. (1999). Two Decades of Research and Development in Transformational Leadership. *European Journal of Work and Organizational Psychology, 8*(1), 9–32. http://citeseerx.ist.psu.edu/viewdoc/download?doi=10.1.1.467.8619&rep=rep1&type=pdf

Bass, B. M., & Riggio, R. E. (2006). *Transformational Leadership* 2nd ed. [ebook]. Lawrence Erlbaum Associates. https://ebookcentral-proquest-com.lib.pepperdine.edu/lib/pepperdine/reader.action?docID=274519

Bass, B. M., & Steidlmeier, P. (1999). Ethics, Character, and Authentic Transformational Leadership Behavior. *The Leadership Quarterly, 10*(2), 181–217. https://doi.org/10.1016/S1048-9843(99)00016-8

Berscheid, E., & Reis, H. (1998). *Attraction and Close Relationships,* 4th ed. Oxford University Press.

Beverly, K. (2016). "Examining the Impact of Leader Member Exchange (LMX) Theory on Employee Engagement and Employee Intent to Stay with an Organization." Doctoral dissertation, Regent University. ProQuest Dissertations and Theses.

Billsberry, J. (2009). "The Social Construction of Leadership Education". *Journal of Leadership Education, 8*(2), 1–9. https://doi.org/10.12806/V8/I2/AB1

Block, P. (2006). Servant-leadership: Creating an alternative future. *The International Journal of Servant-Leadership, 2*(1), 1–578. www.spearscenter.org/docs2010/InternationalJournalofServantLeadership2006.pdf

Bolman, L. G., & Deal, T. E. (2017). *Performing Organizations* 6th ed. A John Wiley and Sons.

Bradberry, T., & Greaves, J. (2009). *Emotional Intelligence 2.0.* TalentSmart.

Braun, V., & Clarke, V. (2006). Using Thematic Analysis in Psychology. *Qualitative Research in Psychology, 3*(2), 77–101. https://doi.org/10.1191/1478088706qp063oa

Brewer, M. B., & Gardner, W. (1996). "Who is this "We"? Levels of Collective Identity and Self Representations". *Journal of Personality and Social Psychology*, *71*(1), 83–93. https://doi.org/10.1037/0022-3514.71.1.83

Brooks, K. (2021). "Banks Could Soon Suffer Massive Wave of Job Losses, Analysts say." *CBS News*. www.cbsnews.com/news/banking-100000-jobs-wells-fargo-analysts-automation/

Brower, H. H., Schoorman, D. F., & Tan, H. H. (2000). "A Model of Relational Leadership: The Integration of Trust and Leader-Member Exchange." *Leadership Quarterly*, *11*(2), 227–250. https://ink.library.smu.edu.sg/lkcsb_research/2431/

Brown, M. H., & Hosking, D. M. (1986). "Distributed Leadership and Skilled Performance as Successful Organization in Social Movements." *Human Relations*, *39*(1), 65–79. https://doi.org/10.1177/001872678603900104

Bryman, A. (1993). "Charismatic Leadership in Business Organizations: Some Neglected Issues." *The Leadership Quarterly*, *4*(3), 289–304. https://doi.org/10.1016/1048-9843(93)90036-S

Burns, J. M. (1978). *Leadership*. Harper & Row.

Carlyle, T. (1841). *On heroes, Hero-Worship, and the Heroic in History*. Compass Circle.

Carter, D. R., Braun, M. T., DeChurch, L. A., & Contractor, N. S. (2015). "Social Network Approaches to Leadership: An Integrative Conceptual Review." *Journal of Applied Psychology*, *100*(3), 597–622. http://dx.doi.org/10.1037/a0038922

Cattell, R. B. (1965). *The Scientific Analysis of Personality*. Penguin Books.

Centers of Disease Control and Prevention (2022). *CDC Museum COVID-19 Timeline*. https://www.cdc.gov/museum/timeline/covid19.html

Chapin, F. S. (1942). "Preliminary Standardization of a Social Impact Scale." *American Sociological Review*, *7*(2), 214–225. https://www.jstor.org/stable/2085176

Chia, R. (1995). "From Modern to Postmodern Organizational Analysis." *Organization Studies*, *16*(4), 579–604. https://doi.org/10.1177/017084069501600406

Coetzer, M. F., Bussin, M., & Geldenhuys, M. (2017). "The Functions of a Servant Leader." *Administrative Science*, *7*(5), 1-32. https://doi.org/10.3390/admsci7010005

Cowley, W. H. (1928). "Three Distinctions in the Study of Leaders." *The Journal of Abnormal and Social Psychology*, *23*(2), 144–157. https://doi.org/10.1037/h0073661

Creswell, J. (2013). *Qualitative Inquiry and Research Design: Choosing Among Five Approaches*. Sage Publications.

Creswell, J. W., & Creswell, D. (2018). *Research design* 5th ed. SAGE.

Dachler, P. H., & Hosking, D. M. (1995a). "The Primacy of Relations in Socially Constructing Organizational Realities." *Management and Organization: Relational Perspectives*, 1–29.

Dachler, P. H., & Hosking, D. M. (1995b). "The Primacy of Relations in Socially Constructing Organizational Realities." *APA PsycInfo*. https://doi.org/https:// psycnet.apa.org/record/1996-97352-001

Dansereau, F., Graen, G., & Haga, W. J. (1975). "A Vertical Dyad Linkage Approach to Leadership Within Formal Organizations: A Longitudinal Investigation of the Role Making Process." *Organizational Behavior and Human Performance*, *13*(1), 46–78. https://calhoun.nps.edu/handle/10945/61488

Dewar, C., Keller, S., Sneader, K., & Stovink, K. (2020). The CEO moment: Leadership for a new era. *McKinsey & Company*, 1–8.

Doll, E. A. 1935. "A Genetic Scale of Social Maturity." *American Journal of Orthopsychiatry*, *5*, 180–188. https://doi.org/10.1111/j.1939-0025.1935. tb06339.x

Drath, W. D. 1990. "Managerial Strengths and Weaknesses as Function of Development of Personal Meaning." *The Journal of Applied Behavior Science*, *26*(4), 483–499.

Drath, W. D. 2001. The D*eep Blue Sea: Rethinking the Source of Leadership*. Jossey-Bass and Center for Creative Leadership.

Eysenck, H. J. 1992. "Four Ways Five Factors are Not Basic." *Personality and Individual Differences, 13*, 667–673.

Fiedler, F. E. 1964. "A Theory of Leadership Effectiveness." In *Advances in Experimental Social Psychology*,edited by L. Berkowitz, 149–190. Academic Press.

Fiol, M. C., Harris, D., & House, R. 1999. "Charismatic Leadership: Strategies for Effecting Social Change." *Leadership Quarterly, 10*(3), 449–282.

Financial Institutions. (n.d.). Statista *Website*. www.statista.com/statistics/193286/ number-of-employees-at-fdic-insured-commercial-banks-in-the-us/

Fiske, D. W. 1949. "Consistency of the Factorial Structures of Personality, Ratings from Different Sources." *Journal of Abnormal and Social Psychology, 44,* 329–344.

French, J., & Raven, B. 1959. The Basis of Social Power. *ReserachGate*. www. researchgate.net/publication/215915730_The_bases_of_social_power

Friedrich, C. J. 1961. "Political Leadership and the Problem of the Charismatic Power." *The Journal of Politics, 23*(1), 3–24. https://www.jstor.org/ stable/2127069

Gajendran, R. S., & Aparna, A. 2012. "Innovation in Globally Distributed Teams: The Role of LMX, Communication Frequency, and Member Influence on Team Decisions." *Journal of Applied Psychology, 97*(6), 1252–1261.

Galoji, S. I., & Jibrin, A. S. 2016. "The Relationship Between Leadership Self-Efficacy and Relational Leadership Behavior". *Journal of Business and African Economy*, *2*(1), 22–34. https://iiardpub.org/get/JBAE/VOL.%202%20 NO.%201%202016/THE%20RELATIONSHIP%20BETWEEN.pdf

Galton, F. 1869. *Hereditary Genius: An Inquiry into its Laws and Consequences*. Macmillan and Co.

Gardner, H. 1983. *Frames of mind: The theory of multiple intelligences*. Basic Books.

Gergen, K. J. 1994. *Toward transformation in social knowledge* 2nd ed. Sage Publications.

Getter, D. E. 2016. "*Overview of commercial (depository) banking and industry conditions* [CRS report R44488]." Congressional Research Services. https:// sgp.fas.org/crs/misc/R44488.pdf

Gill, R. 2011. *Theory and practice of leadership*. Sage Publications

Gilligan, C. 1982. In a different voice: Psychological theory and women's development. *Harvard University Press*, 24–39. www.researchgate.net/ publications/275714105

Gladwell, M. 2008. Outliers. *Hachette Book Group*.

Goffee, R., & Jones, G. 2013. Creating the best workplace on earth. *Harvard Business Review*. https://hbr.org/2013/05/creating-the-best-workplace-on-earth.

Goldberg, L. R. 1981. "Language and Individual Differences: The Search for Universals in Personality Lexicons." In, *Review of personality and social psychology* , L. Wheeler (Ed.), *2*, 141–165. Sage.

Goleman, D. 1995. *Emotional Intelligence* 10th ed. Bantam Books.

Goleman, D. 1998. What Makes a Leader. *Harvard Business Review*.

Goleman, D. 2004. Leadership that Gets Results. *Harvard Business Review*.

Goleman, D, & Boyatzis, R. 2017. "Emotional Intelligence has 12 Elements. Which do you Need to Work on?" *Harvard Business Review*.

Gostin, L. 1991. "Ethical Principles for the Conduct of Human Subject Research: Population-Based Research and Ethics." *Law, Medicine & Health Care, 19*(3–4), 191–201.

Graen, G. B. 2016. "To Share or not to Share Leadership." *ResearchGate*. https:// doi.org/10.13140/RG.2.1.3057.0002

Graen, G. B., & Uhl-Bien, M. 1995. "Relationship-Based Approach to Leadership: Development of Leader-Member Exchange (LMX) Theory of Leadership over 25 years: Applying a Multi-Level Multi-Domain Perspective." *Leadership Quarterly*, *6*(2), 219–247. https://digitalcommons.unl.edu/ managementfacpub/57

Graham, J. W. 1991. "Servant-Leadership in Organizations: Inspirational and Moral." *The Leadership Quarterly*, *2*(2), 105–119. https://doi. org/10.1016/1048-9843(91)90025-W

Greenleaf, R. K. 1977. *A Journey into the Nature of Legitimate Power and Greatness.* Paulist Press.

Grint, K. 2005. "Problems, Problems, Problems: The Social Construction of 'Leadership'." *Human Relations,* 58(11), 1467–1494. https://doi.org/10.1177/0018726705061314

Gronn, P. 2009. Leadership Configurations. *Leadership,* 5(3), 381–394. https://doi.org/10.1177/1742715009337770

Groysberg, B., Kelly, K., & MacDonald, B. (2011). The New Path to the C-suite. *Harvard Business Review.* https://hbr.org/2011/03/the-new-path-to-the-c-suite

Hersey, P., & Blanchard, K. H. 1969. "The Contribution of Cognitive Resources to Leadership Performance." *Journal of Applied Social Psychology, 16,* 532–545.

Hesse, H. 1956. *The Journey to the East.* Peter Owen Publishing.

Hicks, L. 2004. Defining Research with Human Subjects. *CITI Program.* https://www.citiprogram.org/members/index.cfm?pageID=665&ce=1#view

Hogg, M. A. 2001. "A Social Identity Theory of Leadership." *Personality and Social Psychology Review,* 5(3), 184–200. http://citeseerx.ist.psu.edu/viewdoc/download?doi=10.1.1.645.2816&rep=rep1&type=pdf

Hollander, E. P. 1992. "The Essential Interdependence of Leadership and Followership." *Current Directions in Psychological Science,* 1(2), 71–75.

Hollander, E. P. 2010. *American Presidential Leadership: Leader Credit, Follower Inclusion, and Obama's Turn* (For the Conference on "When Far is Near and Near is Far: Exploring 'Distance' in Leader-Follower Relationships," March 6th, 2010, Claremont Graduate University) [American Presidential Leadership]. Baruch College. www.ila-net.org//InducteeMaterials/HollanderLegacy.pdf

Hosking, D. M. 1988. "Organizing, Leadership, and Skillful Process." *Journal of Management Studies,* 25(2), 147–166.

Hosking, D. M., & Pluut, B. 2010. "(Re)constructing Reflexivity: A Relational Constructionist Approach." *The Qualitative Report,* 15(1), 59–75. https://doi.org/10.46743/2160-3715/2010.1140

House, R. J. 1976. *A 1976 theory of charismatic leadership* (Working Paper) [76-06]. Southern Illinois University Fourth Biennial Leadership Symposium.

House, R. J. 1996. "Path-goal theory of leadership: Lessons, legacy, and a reformulated theory." *Leadership, 7,* 323–352.

Hu, H., Jadoul, Q., & Reich, A. 2021. "How Banks can Build Their Future Workforce—Today." *McKinsey & Company.* www.mckinsey.com/industries/financial-services/our-insights/how-banks-can-build-their-future-workforce-today

Hyatt, L. 2017. Narrative Dynamics – A Qualitative Approach. Presentation at the Research Methods Colloquium, Los Angeles, CA.

Judge, T. A., Shaw, J. C., Jackson, C., Scott, B. A., & Rich, B. L. 2007. "Self-Efficacy and Work-Related Performance: The Integral Role of Individual Differences." *Journal of Applied Psychology, 92*(1), 107–127. https://doi.org/10.1037/0021-9010.92.1.107

Kanodia, R., & Sacher, A. 2016. "Trait Theories of Leadership." *International Journal of Science Technology and Management, 5*(12), 121–133. www.ijstm.com/images/short_pdf/1480489811_537ijstm.pdf

Katz, J. H., & Miller, F. A. 2014. "Leaders getting different; Collaboration, the new inclusive workplace, and OD's role." *The Organization Development Practitioner, 46*(3), 40–45.

Katzenbach, J. R., & Smith, D. K. 1999. *The Wisdom of Teams: Creating the High-Performance Organizations*. HarperBusiness.

Kirkpatrick, S. A., & Locke, E. A. 1991. "Leadership: Do Traits Matter?" *Academy of Management Executive, 5*(2), 48–60. https://sites.fas.harvard.edu/~soc186/AssignedReadings/Kirkpatrick-Traits.pdf

Klier, H. T.2009. "From tail fins to hybrids: How Detroit Lost its Dominance." *Federal Reserve Bank of Chicago. Economic Perspectives, Vol. 13*.

Knippenberg, B., Knippenberg, D., Cremer, D. D., & Hogg, M. A. 2005. "Research in Leadership, Self, and Identity: A Sample of the Present and Glimpse of the Future." *The Leadership Quarterly, 16*, 495–499. https://doi.org/10.1016/j.leaqua.2005.06.006

Kotter, J. P. 1990. What leaders really do. *Harvard Business Review*, 103–111.

Kotter, J. P. 1996. *Leading change*. Harvard Business Review Press.

Kotter, J. P. 1995. "Leading change: Why Transformation Efforts Fail." *On Change Management*. Harvard Business Review Press.

Lanaj, K., Foulk, T, & Erez, A. 2019. "Energizing Leaders Via Self-Reflection: A Within-Person Field Experiment." *Journal of Applied Psychology, 104*(1), 1–18. https://doi.org/10.1037/apl0000350

Landis, J. R., & Koch, G. G. 1977. "The Measurement of Observer Agreement for Categorical Data." *Biometrics, 33*, 159–174.

Latham, G. P., & Locke, E. A. 1991. "Self-Regulation Through Goal Setting." *The Academy of Management Review, 50*, 212–247. https://doi.org/10.2307/258875

Lewin, K. 1947. "Frontiers in Group Dynamics: Concept, Method and Reality in Social Science; Social Equilibria and Social Change." *SAGE Journals, 5*–41. https://doi.org/10.1177/001872674700100103

Lick, J., & Bootzin, R. 1975. "Expectancy Factors in the Treatment of Fear: Methodological and Theoretical Issues." *Psychological Bulletin, 82*(6), 917–931. https://doi.org/10.1037/0033-2909.82.6.917

Lincoln, Y. S., & Guba, E. 1986. *Naturalistic Inquiry*. Sage.

Locke, E. A., & Latham, G. P. 1990. *A Theory of Goal Setting and Task Performance*. Prentice-Hall.

Locke, L. F., Spirduso, W. W., & Silverman, S. J. 2013. *Proposals that Work: A Guide for Planning Dissertations and Grant Proposals* 6th ed. SAGE.

Lord, R. G., & Emrich, C. 2001. "Thinking Outside the Box by Looking Inside the Box: Extending Cognitive Revolution in Leadership Research." *Leadership Quarterly, 11*(4), 551–579. https://doi.org/10.1016/S1048-9843(00)00060-6

Lunenburg, F. C. 2010. "Leader-Member Exchange Theory: Another Perspective on the Leadership Process." *International Journal of Management, Business, and Administration, 13*, 1–5.

Macrotrends. n.d. Ford Motor Gross Profit 2010-2023. https://www.macrotrends.net/stocks/charts/F/ford-motor/revenue

Marilena, Z., & Alice, T. 2012. "The Profit and Loss Account Major Tool for the Analysis of the Company's Performance." *Social and Behavioral Sciences, 62*, 382–387. https://doi.org/10.1016/j.sbspro.2012.09.061

Mayer, J. D., & Salovey, P. 1997. "What is Emotional Intelligence?" In , *Emotional development and emotional intelligence: Educational implications* edited by P. Salovey and D. J. Sluyter, 3–34. Basic Books.

McCall, M. W., Lombardo, M. M., & Morrison, A. M. 1988. *Lessons of Experience: How Successful Executives Develop on the Job.* Lexington Books.

McCrae, R. R., & Costa, P. T., Jr. 1987. "Validation of the Five-Factor Model of Personality Across Instruments and Observers." *Journal of Personality and Social Psychology, 52*, 81–90.

Moore, N. 1965. "Behavior Therapy in Bronchial Asthma: A Controlled Study." *Journal of Psychosomatic Research, 9*(3), 257–276. https://doi.org/10.1016/0022-3999(65)90051-6

Moss, F. A., & Hunt, T. 1927. "Are you Socially Intelligent?" *Scientific American, 137*(2), 108–110. www.jstor.org/stable/10.2307/24964691

Murrell, K. L. 1997. "Emergent Theories of Leadership for the Next Century: Towards Relational Concepts." *Organization Development, 15*(3), 35–42.

Norman, W. T. 1967. *2800 Personality Trait Descriptors: Normative Operating Characteristics for a University Population.* Department of Psychology, University of Michigan. http://eric.ed.gov/?id=ED014738

O'Connor, C., & Joffe, H. 2020. "Intercoder Reliability in Qualitative Research: Debates and Practical Guidelines." *International Journal of Qualitative Methods, 19.* http://dx.doi.org.lib.pepperdine.edu/10.1177/1609406919899220

Pajares, F. 1997. "Current Directions in Self-Efficacy Research.",In *Advances in Motivation and Achievement,*Edited by M. Maehr, & P. R. Pintrich Vol. 10, 1–49. JAI Press.

Parker, K., Horowitz, J., & Minkin, R. 2020, . "*How the Coronavirus Outbreak Has—and Hasn't—Changed the Way Americans Work.*" Pew Research Center. www.pewresearch.org/social-trends/2020/12/09/how-the-coronavirus-outbreak-has-and-hasnt-changed-the-way-americans-work/

Patterson, K. 2003. *Servant Leadership: A Theoretical Model* [Doctoral dissertation, Regent University]. Regent University Archive. www.regent.edu/wp-content/uploads/2020/12/patterson_servant_leadership.pdf

Patton, M. Q. 2015. *Qualitative Research 7 Evaluation Methods: Integrating Theory and Practice,* 4ᵗʰ ed. Sage

Paul, G. L. 1966. *Insight vs. Desensitization in Psychotherapy.* Stanford University Press.

Pepperdine University Graduate & Professional Schools Institutional Review Board. (2019). Graduate and Professional Schools IRB. https://community.pepperdine.edu/irb/revised-common-rule/

Power, R. L. 2013. "Leader-Member Exchange Theory in Higher and Distance Education." *The International Review of Research in Open and Distance Learning, 14*(4), 277–234. https://files.eric.ed.gov/fulltext/EJ1017531.pdf

Roberto, M. 2005. *Why Great Leaders Don't Take Yes for an Answer.* Wharton School Publishing.

Roberts, C., & Hyatt, L. 2019. *The Dissertation Journey* 3rd ed. SAGE.

Robinson Bailey, L. 2004. *History and ethical principles.* CITI Program. www.citiprogram.org/members/index.cfm?pageID=665&ce=1#view

Rockstuhl, T. (2012). "Leader-Member-Exchange (LMX) and Culture: A Meta-Analysis of Correlates of LMX Across 23 Countries." *ResearchGate.* https://doi.org/10.1037/a0029978

Russell, R. F., & Stone, G. A. 2002. "A Review of Servant Leadership Attributes: Developing a Practical Model." *Leadership & Organization Development Journal, 23*(3), 145–157. https://psycnet.apa.org/doi/10.1108/01437730210424

Salovey, P., & Mayer, J. D. 1990. "Emotional Intelligence." *Imagination, Cognition and Personality, 9*(3), 185–211. https://doi.org/10.2190/DUGG-P24E-52WK-6CDG

Schyns, B., & Day, D. 2010. "Critique and Review of Leader–Member Exchange Theory: Issues of Agreement, Consensus, and Excellence." *European Journal of Work and Organizational Psychology, 19*(1), 1–29. www.tandfonline.com/doi/abs/10.1080/13594320903024922

Seipp, B. 1991. "Anxiety and Academic Performance: A Meta-Analysis of Findings." *Anxiety Research, 4*(1), 27–41. https://doi.org/10.1080/08917779108248762

Semadar, A., Robins, G., & Ferris, G. 2006. "Comparing the Validity of Multiple Social Effectiveness Constructs in the Prediction of Managerial Job Performance." *Journal of Organizational Behavior, 27*(4), 443–461. https://doi.org/10.1002/job.385

Senge, P. M. 1990. *The Discipline; The Art & Practice of the Learning Organizations* 1st ed. Crown Publishing Group.

Schon, D. A. 1983. The Reflective Practitioner: How Professionals Think in Basic Books, New York.

Shamir, B., House, R. J., & Arthur, M. B. 1993. "The Motivational Effects of Charismatic Leadership: A Self-Concept-Based Theory." *Organization Science*, *4*(4), 599–594. www.jstor.org/stable/2635081

Shavelson, R. J., & Bolus, R. 1982. "Self-Concept: The Interplay of Theory and Models." *Journal of Educational Psychology*, *71*(1), 3–17. https://www.rand.org/content/dam/rand/pubs/papers/2009/P6607.pdf

Smith, E. R., & Henry, S. (1996). "An In-Group Becomes Part of the Self: Response Time Evidence." *Personality and Social Psychology Bulletin*, *22*(6), 635–642. https://doi.org/10.1177/0146167296226008

Smith, P. A. 1987. The U.S. Automakers' Reaction to the Japanese. *Vol 2* (4). https://scholarworks.uni.edu/draftings/vol2/iss4/3

Spears, L. C. (2010). "Character and Servant Leadership: Ten Characteristics of Effective, Caring Leaders." *The Journal of Virtues & Leadership*, *1*(1), 25–30.

Srivastava, P., & Hopwood, N. (2009). "A Practical Iterative Framework for Qualitative Data Analysis." *International Journal of Qualitative Methods*, *8*(1), 76–84. https://doi.org/10.1177%2F160940690900800107

Stajkovic, A. D., & Luthans, F. (1998). "Self-Efficacy and Work-Related Performance: A Meta-Analysis." *Psychological Bulletin*, *124*(2), 240–261. https://doi.org/10.1037/0033-2909.124.2.240

Stogdill, R. M. 1948. *Personal Factors Associated With Leadership: A Survey of the Literature*. Free Press.

Tajfel, H. 1972, "Social Categorization. English Manuscript of "La Catégorisation Sociale." In, *Introduction a la Psychologie Sociale*, 1, 272–302. Larousse.

Tan, T. Q. 2019. "Principles of Inclusion, Diversity, Access, and Equity." *The Journal of Infectious Diseases*, *220*(2), 30–32. https://doi.org/10.1093/infdis/jiz198

Thorndike, E. L. 1920. Intelligence and Its Uses. *Harper's Magazine*, *140*, 227–235. www.gwern.net/docs/iq/1920-thorndike.pdf

Thorpe, R., Gold, J., & Lawler, J. 2011. "Locating Distributive Leadership." *International Journal of Management Reviews*, *13*(3), 239–250. https://doi.org/10.1111/j.1468-2370.2011.00303.x

Tracey, B. J., & Hinkin, T. R. 1998. "Transformational Leadership or Effective Managerial Practices?" *Group & Organization Management*, *23*(3), 220–236. https://doi.org/doi:10.1177/1059601198233002

Tucker, R. C. 1968. "The Theory of Charismatic Leadership." *American Academy of Arts & Sciences*, *97*(3), 731–756. http://jstor.com/stable/20023840

Uhl-Bien, M. 2006. "Relational Leadership Theory: Exploring the Social Processes of Leadership and Organizing." *The Leadership Quarterly*, *17*, 654–676. https://doi.org/10.10.1016/j..leaqua.2006.10.007

Van Dierendonck, D. 2011. "Servant Leadership: A Review and Synthesis." *Journal of Management*, *37*(4), 1228–1261. https://doi.org/10.1177/0149206310380462

Von Glasersfeld, E. 1985. "Reconstructing the Concept of Knowledge." *Archives de Psychologie,* *53*(204), 91–101. https://psycnet.apa.org/record/1986-07979-001

Von Glasersfeld, E. 1989. "Cognition, Construction of Knowledge, and Teaching." *History, Philosophy, and Science Teaching, 80*(1), 121–140. www.jstor.org/stable/20116670

The Wall Street Journal. (2021). *"Wall Street CEOs Say Working From Home Isn't Working"* [Podcast]. Wall Street Journal. www.wsj.com/podcasts/the-journal/wall-street-ceos-say-working-from-home-isnt-working/e4f0de44-4d2e-4cd9-8e8c-0d569bae291d

Weber, M. 1947. *The Theory of Social and Economic Organizations.* Oxford University Press.

Weber, M. 1958. "The Three Types of Legitimate Rule." *Berkeley Publications in Society and Institutions, 4*(1), 1–11.

Wechsler, D. 1943. "Non-Intellective Factors in General Intelligence." *The Journal of Abnormal and Social Psychology, 38*(1), 101–103. https://doi.org/10.1037/h0060613

Wechsler, D. 1958. *The Measurement and Appraisal of Adult Intelligence 4ᵗʰ ed.* Williams & Wilkins.

Wood, R. E., & Bandura, A. 1989. "Social Cognitive Theory of Organizational Management." *Academy of Management Review, 14*(3), 361–384. www.jstor.org/stable/258173

Yukl, G. 1999. "An Evaluation of Conceptual Weaknesses in Transformational and Charismatic Leadership Theories." *The Leadership Quarterly, 10*(2), 285–305. https://doi.org/10.1016/S1048-9843(99)00013-2

Yukl, G. 2010. *Leadership in Organizations 7th ed.* Pearson.

About the Author

Dr. Rocky Bandzeladze has 25 years of experience in driving growth and transformation across diverse organizations. His expertise in organizational strategy and cultural transformation is grounded in relational leadership, a practice that emphasizes a collective effort to cultivate environments where leaders, followers, and their organizations can thrive together. Having successfully led both start-ups and large financial institutions, Dr. Bandzeladze believes that robust, long-term organizational performance is intricately linked to a trust-based, engaging culture.

Born in the Republic of Georgia, Dr. Bandzeladze arrived in the United States at 19 with just $180—the money left after buying a plane ticket with the proceeds from selling his family's only asset, their car. His humble upbringing and multicultural background shape his unique insights into leadership and decision-making. Inspired by leaders who build trust and authentic connections, he is dedicated to creating people-centered cultures that drive sustainable organizational success.

Index

www.ingramcontent.com/pod-product-compliance
Lightning Source LLC
Chambersburg PA
CBHW061335220326
41599CB00026B/5193